Debating Supreme Court Decisions

Schenck v. United States and the Freedom of Speech Debate

Debating Supreme Court Decisions

Jodi Icenoggle

Enslow Publishers, Inc.

40 Industrial Road	PO Box 38
Box 398	Aldershot
Berkeley Heights, NJ 07922	Hants GU12 6BP
USA	UK

http://www.enslow.com

Library of Congress Cataloging-in-Publication Data

Icenoggle, Jodi, 1967-
    Schenck v. United States and the freedom of speech debate : debating Supreme
Court decisions / Jodi Icenoggle.— 1st ed.
       p. cm. — (Debating Supreme Court decisions)
    Includes bibliographical references and index.
    ISBN 0-7660-2392-3
    1. Freedom of speech—United States—Juvenile literature. 2. Schenck, Charles—
Trials, litigation, etc.—Juvenile literature. I. Title: Schenck versus United States.
II. Title. III. Series.
KF4772.Z9I24 2005
323.44'3'0973—dc22

                          2004028117

Printed in the United States of America

10 9 8 7 6 5 4 3 2 1

To Our Readers: We have done our best to make sure that all Internet Addresses in this
book were active and appropriate when we went to press. However, the author and publisher
have no control over and assume no liability for the material available on those Internet sites
or on other Web sites they may link to. Any comments or suggestions can be sent by e-mail
to comments@enslow.com or to the address on the back cover.

Illustration Credits: AP/Wide World, p. 71; Digital Vision, p. 89; Hemera Image
Express, p. 2; Library of Congress, pp. 17, 27, 39, 51, 62, 83; St. Louis Post-
Dispatch, p. 9.

Cover Illustrations: Background, Artville; photograph, EyeWire Images.

Contents

chapter 1

What Is Free Speech?

What is free speech?

This is a simple question, but one that leads to others: Should *all* speech be free? What limits are placed on speech? Who decides those limits?

You are a student working on a school newspaper. You and the rest of the student staff work hard on an issue. Two pages of it are removed from print by the principal. Is this a question of free speech?

Students in Hazelwood East High School in St. Louis, Missouri, thought it was. In 1983, the students planned a six-page final issue of *Spectrum*, the school paper. They included a two-page spread about issues of special interest to teens. The topics included juvenile delinquency, teenage pregnancy, birth control, divorce, abortion, and teenage marriages.[1]

The principal decided the special-interest topics were too sensitive and inappropriate for younger students. He was also concerned about the anonymity of some of the quoted sources. He had the two pages deleted from the paper. The students did not know two pages had been taken out until the paper was printed. They objected to his decision, believing that the principal violated their First Amendment rights. So they took their dispute to the court system.[2]

The Constitution guarantees the right to free speech; in order to maintain a democracy, ideas must be exchanged freely.[3] Freedom of speech implies freedom to communicate without interference from the government. Some believe this covers freedom of the press (newspapers). Many times, this freedom is intertwined with the right to gather peaceably, the right to petition the government, and the freedom of religion. These five rights together are considered freedom of expression.[4]

No one knows exactly what the Founding Fathers intended when they drafted the Bill of Rights, which lists the first ten constitutional amendments. State courts decide whether state laws are unconstitutional. In the Hazelwood case, the students won at the circuit court level; that court held that the principal had wrongly censored the newspaper. (A circuit court is a federal court

U.S. Constitution

Amendment 1: Freedom of Religion, Speech, and the Press; Rights of Assembly and Petition

Congress shall make no law respecting an establishment of religion, or prohibiting the free exercise thereof; or abridging the freedom of speech, or of the press, or the right of the people peaceably to assemble, and to petition the Government for a redress of grievances.

that rules on cases that involve federal issues, such as free speech.)

Sometimes, people do not like decisions of the district courts and appeal their cases to the Supreme Court of the United States. As the highest court in our country, it can uphold (agree with) or overturn (disagree with) lower court decisions. Hazelwood school officials asked the Supreme Court to review the case. The Court reversed the lower court decision, saying that school officials had the right to control student expression, as long as that control had a valid educational purpose and was reasonable. Because the school paper was part of the school's curriculum, its contents were subject to approval. The principal's censorship was acceptable to the Supreme Court.

Spectrum was a school-sponsored paper, so

school authorities could determine the content. What students write in the school paper represents the school. They were not simply expressing their own opinions. Those articles were presented to other students and parents, some of whom might think the school encourages or shares those views. The students' First Amendment rights were not violated by the principal's decision to delete two pages from the final issue, said the Supreme Court.

It is imperative to protect individual rights without infringing on the rights of others. This delicate balance at times seems straightforward. At other times, it is hard to distinguish who is right and who is wrong. The courts make decisions and answer certain questions.

For example, one student in your school might tell his friends that his English class is boring. Another student might be failing English, so he lies about his teacher to get the teacher in trouble. The first student's speech is harmless. He is stating his opinion. The second student is telling lies that could harm the teacher's reputation and job. Because he is speaking, versus writing, the second student could be guilty of slander (similar to libel, but the damage is done orally).

The First Amendment right to free speech does not apply to libel or slander. Sometimes it is difficult to determine when someone is stating his

Cathy Kuhlmeier holds a copy of Spectrum, the school newspaper that was censored by the principal because he objected to some of the articles. The Supreme Court upheld the school district's right to control the paper's content.

or her opinion and when he or she is guilty of libel or slander. If a student at school does not want to vote for a candidate running for student council, that student can say she is not confident the candidate would do a good job. She is stating her opinion and not attacking the candidate. If, instead, the student were to give speeches or print flyers saying that the candidate lies, cheats, and steals, the student could be guilty of libel and slander because she is telling falsehoods to damage the candidate's character.

The Idea of Free Speech

The idea of free speech began centuries ago in ancient Greece. Athens, long considered the greatest city-state in Greece, allowed its citizens the widest range of freedom at that time, including that of speech. But that freedom was permitted only to men of the elite class.

The idea of free speech slowly evolved, gaining and losing momentum with subsequent societies, always stirring up controversy. Different countries defined free speech differently, and many looked at this freedom as harmful to society. Many governments did not allow citizens to criticize, because they feared losing control of their people. This was the case during the American Revolution. England and its monarchy did not allow people to speak freely and punished those who disobeyed the king and parliament.

American colonists, who were ruled by the king, did not like this restriction. They wanted to speak their opinions, no matter what those opinions were. Men were accused of sedition (revolt against a ruling government) if they disagreed with a law or a decision the king made. Colonists broke away from England, in part, to gain greater personal freedom for themselves. The right to free speech was guaranteed by the U.S. Constitution. The men who drafted the Constitution wanted to ensure that Americans could criticize the government without fear of punishment. But only seven years after the Bill of Rights was passed, the Sedition Act of 1798 outlawed criticism of the United States government, which was controlled by the Federalist Party. Men were jailed, and the act expired in 1801.

Today, if someone disagrees with the President or Congress, that person can say so. Free speech protects a person's right to disagree. However, that right does not include sedition. A person may disagree but may not incite violence against the government by using speech that encourages revolt.

Forms of Communication

People communicate through speech, through the written word (as in newspapers), through symbols (flags, bumper stickers, T-shirts), and through actions (such as marches, protests, and meetings). Should *all* communication be covered by the First Amendment?

What does the Constitution mean? Did the drafters intend to protect *all* speech or only that speech that is useful to the good of society? Many feel the drafters were mainly concerned with the government gaining too much power and taking away citizens' rights.

Let's begin with the oral word. Free speech covers what is said. But offensive statements (insults and epithets), defamation (false speech that aims to destroy a person's reputation, including libel and slander), hate speech (using race, ethnic background, religion, gender, or sexual preference to incite violence toward the person or group being talked about), insults (name-calling), and obscenities (swearing) are all spoken words. After all, speech and action are tightly linked, and sometimes it is difficult to tell the difference between the two.

How do freedom of speech and freedom of press relate to one another? The two freedoms are closely linked because both include the right to speak and the right to be heard. Freedom of speech and press are imperative to a democracy because they allow people to gather information from a variety of sources, make decisions, and tell the government of those decisions. Freedom of speech and press ensure that the government does not dictate ideas to its citizens. Rather, citizens can dictate truth to the government by sharing ideas.

The principle of a free press includes the absence of prior restraint. (Prior restraint means to stop a message before it is expressed.) Under First Amendment protection, the press is free to print anything, without government approval. But the press can be held liable for libel or other exceptions to free speech. In other words, if they print something that is obscene, they can be prosecuted. All opinions are printed. The government can limit what is in newspapers, to the extent of barring obscenities. And in broadcast media, indecency is regulated as well.

Most speech is protected under the First Amendment, and that extends to the press. But broadcast media, such as television, has less protection than printed material.[5] Jerome A. Barron, author of *Freedom of the Press For Whom?*, believes that true freedom of press is an ideal, not an attainable reality.[6] Sometimes prior restraint is acceptable as a last resort, such as when it is used in the form of a gag order to ensure a fair trial, or when it is used to prevent national security breaches. One example is the embedded journalists during the Iraq war who had to have their reports OK'd by the military. Protection from prior restraint does not eliminate a publisher's responsibility from legal penalties that might result from publishing certain information.[7] Authors or editors can be punished following publication. Journalists must be careful to check sources and be truthful.

Both speech and press have to weigh the good of society against an individual's right to complete freedom of expression. Supreme Court Justice Oliver Wendell Holmes once said that a person is not allowed to shout false alarms of danger and cause panic, as in a theater.[8] A person's individual freedom to say anything is weighed against the good of society. If a person falsely shouts "Fire!" in a crowded theater and causes other people harm, he or she could be punished.

Conflicting Standards

Members in a society are expected to act with respect toward others while maintaining basic personal freedoms. This seems logical, but each person defines free speech differently. One person might not find the terms "tard" or "queer" offensive. Another person might. Can the first person say the offensive terms to the second person, claiming his right to free speech? Or can the second person insist the first person not use those terms?

In 1982, John Wallace, an African-American

administrator in Virginia, tried to remove the book *The Adventures of Huckleberry Finn* by Mark Twain from his school's curriculum. Mr. Wallace was offended by the book's use of the word "nigger" 160 times. Wallace's argument for censoring the book was that black children who read it would be offended and think less of themselves. However, Dr. Kenneth Clark, also African American, said that he discovered this book when he was twelve years old and loved it because it was a great story. He did not feel a need to remove the book, because he was not offended by the use of that word. He did not focus on the word; he focused on the story.[9]

Randall Kennedy, a Harvard law professor and author of *Nigger: The Strange Career of a Troublesome Word*, agrees. He wrote his book in order to investigate the term. Today, people are reluctant to use it, but he can remember a time when it was used (insultingly) on the floors of the U.S. House of Representatives and the Senate. The word makes people uncomfortable and is a powerful racial insult, but he wants people to remember it. It has caused pain, and still does.[10] Today, it is used in African-American popular culture in movies and rap songs.

Those drafting amendments to our Constitution tried to protect the interests of the citizens of a fledgling country, never dreaming the size or scope of the future population. Thomas Jefferson warned that amendments were necessary to keep up with changes in society.[11] Today, the words of two hundred years ago must be applied to a modern society through legal interpretation of the Constitution. That is accomplished through the courts. Alexander Hamilton once said that the judicial branch was the least dangerous branch of the government and that it protected the will of the people.[12]

Symbolic speech is also known as expressive conduct. Symbolic speech uses actions that are a message even without spoken words. Some examples are burning a draft card or burning an American flag. Symbolic speech can be passive, such as displaying a symbol, or can be conduct, such as wearing low-cut jeans to protest a school policy against such clothing. Symbolic speech is protected by the First Amendment, as long as the conduct connected with the idea does not break any laws or violate other rights.

Many men died during the Revolutionary War. They died for freedom from the tyranny of an English king, freedom from religious persecution, and freedom to disagree with those in power. Freedom of speech encourages discussion. How far a person can take that disagreement is determined by laws. A group of students in school might decide to shout insults at gay students, claiming their

This drawing shows Huckleberry Finn with Jim, an escaped slave. Mark Twain's book has been challenged in schools because some people are offended by its language.

action is a form of protest and protected by the First Amendment.

Many people have challenged free speech. Some feel limits must be placed on a person's rights, and that all hate speech ("All niggers should be strung up") and offensive statements ("Why don't you leave, you dirty ho") be punishable.[13] One way to think of offensive speech is to look at the action involved. Speech that also uses action is known as speech-plus. The action can be literally physical, such as a march or demonstration. Or it can be more symbolic, like burning a draft card. Sometimes, the action part of speech-plus can mean the speech has less First Amendment protection. Many offensive words are selected because of their emotional value. Some people believe that by placing limits on these types of speech, violence can be avoided.

Others feel there should be no limits to free speech and all statements—including hate speech, insults, and offensive statements—should be allowed so that society can discuss all issues. According to this reasoning, a racist has the right to say anything, because if a racist is limited, so is someone who is not racist. As former secretary of state Colin Powell has said, "Free speech is intended to protect the controversial and even outrageous word. . . ."[14]

After looking at this debate and tracing the

issue throughout American history, you can form your opinion about the First Amendment. You will participate in moot court, a type of mock legal proceeding. Perhaps you will better appreciate the right guaranteed by a few words that were added to our Constitution: this right of freedom of speech.

chapter 2

History of Free Speech

According to Samuel Noah Kramer, author of *The Sumerians: Their History, Culture, and Character*, the word "freedom" was first used in the twenty-fourth century B.C. King Urukagina of the Sumerian city of Lagash took away the government's power to seize donkeys, sheep, or other property. Tax collectors no longer existed.[1] The poor did not beg for food because rations were allotted to the less fortunate citizens. Those jailed under false charges were freed. Priests could not exploit the helpless to fill their pockets.[2] However, Urukagina did not allow freedom of speech.[3]

This liberty was not granted to citizens until the Athenians did so during the Archaic period (800–400 B.C.). Athens boasted a reputation of great personal freedom, attracting artists, teachers, statesmen, and philosophers, who all wished to express themselves freely.

Although Athens allowed freedom of speech, it was not uniform throughout society. Only men were granted this right. Women and children were not considered citizens; therefore, they were not allowed freedom of speech. Neither were slaves.

During the golden age of Pericles, from 443 to 429 B.C., this freedom reached its peak. Pericles cultivated Athens into a magnificent city of the ancient world by making it a center of literature and art. He encouraged each citizen to take part in government. Greeks believed that individuals were the strength of society. As long as people obeyed laws, they encouraged individuality. Athens is considered a model for today's government. But Greek society had limitations. Athenians did not allow slander (especially of the dead), sedition, or blasphemy (irreverent or disrespectful speech about the sacred).

Socrates, a philosopher, lived from 470 to 399 B.C. His views and teachings frightened the political and religious leaders of Athens because he talked about new gods and because he did not always agree with politicians or city officials. Many suspected him of corrupting the morals of the youth. Socrates was put on trial. He was allowed to give a speech in his defense, but he failed to convince the judges that he was innocent.

He was given the choice of silencing his views or dying. Socrates chose to die. He drank a cup of hemlock, a poison that was routinely used to carry out death sentences. Many scholars feel Socrates accepted his death sentence as a way to protest the limits of free speech in Athens.

The early history of Rome was similar to that of Athens—certain citizens were allowed a high degree of freedom of speech, though Roman law did not permit slander or sedition. Freedom of speech was reserved for members of the Senate. And only the elite could read and write. The shift from democracy in Rome to one-man rule marked a dark period for free speech. No tolerance was shown for people who spoke against the government during the reign of Tiberius, who ruled from 14 to 37 A.D.

Attitudes prevalent in the Mediterranean world were slowly adopted in Europe during the Middle Ages. From 300 A.D. to 1500 A.D., people struggled to assert rights for themselves, particularly from the medieval Church, which did not believe in freedom of speech.[4] People demanded a written statement, guaranteeing their rights, from their rulers. People wanted limits placed on government control.

England: The Magna Carta and Beyond

In England, what began as the fight for freedom of speech proved to be the core of a larger battle for individual freedom.

In 1215, King John of England ruled ruthlessly over his subjects. He extended his powers beyond what his barons considered reasonable. He insulted the Church, his barons, and all free men (nobility). He demanded high taxes to pay for costly wars. Those who did not pay were punished or killed. He changed his mind frequently in deciding the fate of those who were in jail. There did not seem to be any reason to his justice. However, those willing to pay large sums to the king oftentimes received a favorable ruling.

The barons demanded that the king sign a charter, the Magna Carta, listing specific promises he vowed to not break. The Magna Carta is considered a landmark bill in the field of human rights, although it did not begin as such. It was a list of concessions the king had to agree to or face a rebellion by those he ruled. Despite his objections, King John signed it on June 15, 1215. This bill placed limits on the king, who had to follow common law before punishing anyone or establishing a new tax. The Magna Carta also gave the nobility specific freedoms. For the first time, a king's power was limited, in writing. Realizing that free debate was necessary for democratic thinking, the English considered this to be a basic charter of civil liberties for all people.

During the sixteenth through the eighteenth centuries, people used the issue of freedom of speech to attain a more democratic form of government. At that time, every press had to be licensed. There was a limit to the number of presses allowed by the queen. Elizabeth controlled what was printed and distributed, and therefore she censored all written materials through this licensing. The poet John Milton published his famous *Areopagitica* in 1644, calling for an end to licensing presses in England and suggesting unrestricted access to all writings, without censorship of government or authority.[5] The work was printed without a license, making it illegal.[6] His action resulted in significant bills of rights to be formulated, although it took another half century for licensing to end in England.

The English Bill of Rights, in 1689, granted Englishmen the following freedoms: to bear arms, to elect members of Parliament (the legislative body that was first used in the thirteenth century), to legal trials, and to freedom of speech in Parliament. It also granted them freedom from cruel and unusual punishments and from unjust taxes. This bill moved the British government toward a constitutional monarchy, meaning that the king and/or queen of England had less power over the common people. This bill redefined the role of the English monarch.

Before the English Bill of Rights, the monarch, or ruler of the country, could impose any tax, without the approval of Parliament, which is similar to

Congress. The common people were not allowed to vote for members of Parliament until the Bill of Rights. Subjects could not voice their opinion about any tax or law. People were fined or jailed without a legal trial. Sometimes people were put to death for minor offenses. This bill was a step toward a more balanced government, one that granted rights to the people of the country.

The Declaration of the Rights of Man and of the Citizen, from the French Revolution of 1789, declared freedom of speech as the people's right. Drafted by Emmanuel Sieyes, it was a fundamental document of French constitutional history.[7] Those forming this document were influenced by the Declaration of Independence, which established America as a separate nation from England on July 4, 1776. The French included in their list of "inalienable rights" the right to freedom of speech. This had a profound effect on thought and government action throughout the nineteenth century.

Free Speech in America

Printing presses were brought to the American colonies in the 1600s, but each press was strictly controlled by censors and could only print religious items. The first paper started in 1679, but it was suppressed by the government after one issue. Early newspapers ran into government interference, because the papers dared to discuss politics. A second paper, the *Boston News-Letter*, did not appear in the colonies until 1704, and it contained financial and foreign news, as well as vital statistics. Licenses were needed for printing presses, and those who owned the presses were under constant attack and fear of jail for printing anything that made the English government uncomfortable.

In 1735, a German immigrant named John Peter Zenger was jailed for seditious libel, the printing of criticism of the government. Zenger printed anonymous articles in the *New York Weekly Journal* that criticized the governor. Zenger refused to reveal the names of those who wrote the articles. He was threatened with death, but his lawyers—including Alexander Hamilton— argued that truth should be a defense for seditious libel. He was acquitted. After his trial, very few people were accused of seditious libel, but licensing continued.[8]

During the American Revolution, each of the state constitutions guaranteed free expression. That liberty was one of the biggest reasons the Americans broke free from England. The United States Constitution, in its original form, would have been refused by the states. The promise of adding amendments to the document, including freedom of speech, convinced many states to approve the Constitution and ratify the document as this country's form of government.

The Constitution of the United States was drafted during the Constitutional Convention of May 25 through September 17, 1787. When the first Congress convened on March 4, 1789, those in attendance had to deal with amendments to the Constitution. Some delegates voted in favor of the Constitution, but they insisted that amendments be added as soon as possible. Of great

Alexander Hamilton gestures at the judge in this depiction of the trial of John Peter Zenger, a newspaper editor whom Hamilton defended successfully in 1735. This landmark trial established the concept that truth was a defense against seditious libel.

concern were freedom of speech and of the press. More states wanted freedom of the press than of speech. Thomas Jefferson said, "Were it left to me to decide whether we should have a government without newspapers, or newspapers without a government, I should not hesitate a moment to prefer the latter."[9] The Constitution was ratified and became effective in 1789, giving birth to the supreme law of a new country: the United States of America.

The Bill of Rights

At first, 124 amendments were proposed by the states; Congress reduced them to twelve. Ten of the twelve were passed by the states and became the Bill of Rights. The Bill of Rights was ratified on December 15, 1791, as a safeguard against government intrusion into personal rights. The delegates who drafted the Bill of Rights were deeply concerned about government growth and wanted to avoid the situation in England: a monarch that allowed few personal freedoms. They used words directly from the Magna Carta in drafting the Bill of Rights.

After the Bill of Rights was ratified and approved, the First Amendment guaranteed the freedom of press, which meant the federal government had no power to license presses. It also meant that ordinary people would be able to judge for themselves about news, instead of relying on censored reports from the elite. The press is the only private business given constitutional protection. Originally, the Bill of Rights applied only to the federal government.

The First Amendment guarantees, among other things, the right to free speech. Then came the inevitable question: Is all speech worthy of protection? Americans are free to say, write, or print just about anything. Courts decide limits on freedom of speech, and sometimes, a person's freedom of speech is curtailed for the good of society.

Since the writing of the Constitution and the adoption of the Bill of Rights, some additional laws have been passed by the United States to clarify the difference between protected speech and potentially harmful speech.

In 1798, Congress passed the Alien and Sedition Acts, making it a criminal offense to encourage opposition to the federal government. Freedom of speech was limited by passage of this act.

Patriotic intolerance during World War I resulted in the passage by Congress of the Espionage Act of 1917, to prevent speech that had the intent to cause sabotage or interfere with military operations. It was amended in 1940 and 1970 and is still in force.

Since then, numerous court cases have brought the issue of free speech to the forefront of debate. Many cases have reached the Supreme Court, where decisions have been made defining free speech.

Today, Congress is passing new laws to define free speech in cyberspace. One side believes everything online is protected by the First Amendment. Another side believes the government needs to regulate content for the Internet. One issue is obscenity and minors being exposed to pornography. By protecting the youngest members of society, will adults who do not want or need that protection be restricted?

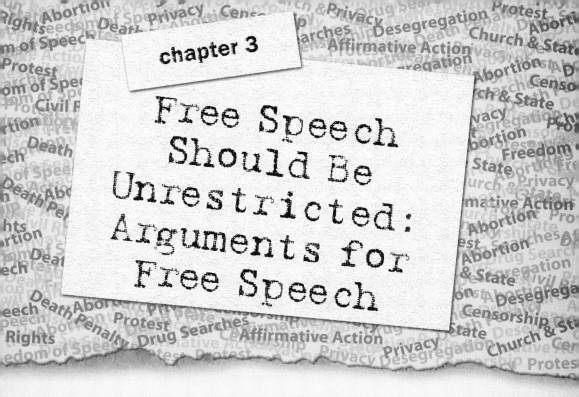

chapter 3

Free Speech Should Be Unrestricted: Arguments for Free Speech

Proponents of pure free speech use several arguments to support their views. We are, in this country, free to say anything, they claim; the act of speaking cannot be prohibited. They note that government *can* punish people after they have said something that breaks a law.

The Self-Fulfillment Argument

Some feel that self-fulfillment is the core of the First Amendment, and it involves both speaking and listening to unrestricted speech.[1] Thomas I. Emerson, a professor of law at Yale, first used this argument in 1966, in *The System of Freedom of Expression*. In it, he argues that individuals have the right to form opinions on any subject and to communicate them to others.[2] Self-fulfillment proponents feel that art, movies, and literary works should be protected because of an individual's right to self-fulfillment. Emerson believed that a distinction had to be made between conduct that consisted of expression and conduct that consisted of action. He felt expression was freely allowed, but action could be controlled.[3]

For example, a student at your school hands out pamphlets, stating his opinion about an upcoming school function. He is doing this because the topic is very important to him and he is trying to achieve self-fulfillment.

Court case: **Cohen** *v.* **California** *(1971).* Shocking language is protected by the Constitution as long as it is not legally obscene or directed at a specific person.[4] Paul Robert Cohen wore a jacket containing an offensive message about the draft into a state courtroom.[5] Because people saw the jacket, he was convicted of disturbing the peace. He did not say anything or cause a disturbance, so he challenged the conviction.[6] He claimed the words on his jacket protested the Vietnam War. Those who did not like the words could have left the hallway or looked the other direction, Cohen said. He claimed that he was not invading the privacy of others because he was not forcing anyone to read his jacket or stand next to him.[7] His conviction was overturned by the Supreme Court, supporting open debate. The significance of this ruling was the narrowing of the definition of fighting words: words directed to another person to create a danger.[8] It also narrowed the definition of obscenity. It showed that shocking language has two meanings. One is cognitive, which expresses ideas. One is emotional, which is personal. States cannot remove certain words from the public's vocabulary simply because those words might be offensive. The Court feared that if words were banned, ideas would soon follow.[9]

The Marketplace Argument

A second argument for free speech is that of the marketplace. This means that ideas will compete with each other, much like products for sale. Any idea should be given a chance to prove itself worthy in society. Good ideas will prevail. Bad ideas will fail. By refusing to listen to certain ideas, society may overlook something of value.[10] The origins of this argument can be traced to John Stuart Mill, author of *On Liberty*; John Milton, author of *Areopagitica* (1644); and Thomas Jefferson, who believed in the freedom to speak and publish.

The marketplace argument is based on three principles: (1) what the majority of people believe to be true may not be; (2) truth needs to be tested; and (3) all opinion contains some truth to the person who believes it.[11] Supreme Court Justice Oliver

Wendell Holmes did not agree with every view or opinion, but he believed in the marketplace. How could the government of a country that was founded on revolution restrict any speech? he asked.[12]

Mill proposed one of the first and most famous liberal defenses of free speech in 1859: Any doctrine should be protected by free speech, no matter how objectionable the content. The only reason to limit a person's speech is to prevent harm to others.[13]

Freedom of the Press For Whom? author Jerome A. Barron agrees that our society should have faith in the marketplace of ideas. Barron believes all ideas should be voiced.[14] Some proponents of the marketplace point to the words in our Constitution: *Congress shall make no law.* No law means no law. Period.[15]

Try applying this theory to your life by answering the following question: Do students have the right to swear while walking through the halls at school? Words might be shocking, and some students might not want to hear them. Using the marketplace theory, students would be able to use swear words, as long as the words did not promote violence and the students' conduct was not disruptive. Those students who did not like the words could leave the conversation or find another place to be.

Court case: **Texas Beef Group** *v.* **Winfrey** *(1996).* Texas cattle ranchers sued Oprah Winfrey after an episode of her talk show discussed mad cow disease. In it, she said she would never eat another hamburger again. The ranchers said that her comment, along with editing of the episode, caused the price of cattle to plummet, costing them $11 million. A Texas jury decided that Winfrey had not defamed the cattle industry. She stated her opinion about beef, and that was protected by the First Amendment.[16] Neither she nor her production company tried to damage the cattle industry. After the verdict, Winfrey said, "Free speech . . . rocks!"[17] Ranchers appealed to the U.S. Court of Appeals for the Fifth Circuit, and the outcome was the same: Oprah Winfrey was not responsible for the fall in cattle prices. She and the expert on her show were stating their opinions and were protected.[18] Some feel that the ranchers sued her because she has a lot of money, and they gambled that she would settle out of court with them.[19] Winfrey has said since the trials that she will continue to state her opinions but will be more careful to make sure viewers know it is her opinion, not something she is stating as fact. In 2002, a U.S. district judge threw out a lingering lawsuit against Winfrey by the beef producers.[20]

The Worthwhile-Speech Argument

A third argument for free speech was proposed by Zechariah Chafee, Jr., a professor of law at Harvard

University. In 1941, he published a landmark study, *Free Speech in the United States*. He believed in protecting speech that serves the social interest, or worthwhile speech, and limiting nonessential speech, or worthless speech (such as profanity or defamation). He saw worthless speech as contributing nothing to society and saw no constitutional objection to punishing such speech. He placed greater value on social speech, or speech that helps citizens be informed on public issues. Chafee believed the only limits on speech are when a true danger to the public is imminent.[21] However, a person's *individual* speech can be limited if it serves no social purpose.[22] In other words, if a person is speaking about politics, that speech should be protected. If that person is talking about something important to him or her, other than politics, it may or may not be protected. Chafee was the first to implement this two-level system of free speech, and he was an advocate of the clear and present danger rule. This rule allows free speech until there is a real danger that is both obvious and immediate.[23] Fighting words cause acts of violence to an individual and, under Chafee's argument, would be worthless speech.[24]

For example, according to Chafee's reasoning, all obscenities—such as calling the principal an obscene name—would fall under worthless speech. But speech serving a social interest, such as demanding why the principal changed a policy, would be protected.

*Court case: **Miller** v. **California** (1973).* Marvin Miller was convicted of distributing sexually explicit brochures. A new test was made by the Supreme Court: If an average person finds a work lewd, and a work is sexually offensive, lacks literary, artistic, political, or scientific value, then a work is considered obscene.[25] If a brochure, a book, or a movie is offensive to most people, even if it has some redeeming social value, it may not enjoy First Amendment protection.[26] This test was developed to limit the number of obscenity cases reaching the Supreme Court. The Miller test was objective, using community standards to determine a work's value. This court case narrowed the material that could be protected under the First Amendment.[27]

The Self-Government Argument

A fourth argument for free speech is self-government. Alexander Meiklejohn, former president of Amherst College, saw freedom of speech as essential for citizens to retain control over government.[28] He wrote *Free Speech and Its Relation to Self-Government* in 1948. He stated that it is a citizen's duty to participate in politics in a democracy.[29] Meiklejohn believed there were two very different kinds of speech: political (speech regarding government or public issues) and private, which can have limitations, according to the due process clause. This clause ensures that the laws used to punish people are fair and equal to all. He believed in absolute protection for political speech and limited protection for private speech (speech not part of the democratic process).[30] Unless there is an immediate danger, government cannot restrict political speech.[31] Everything worth saying should be said. Ideas should be expressed freely, without fear of punishment, in order for people to make informed decisions about their government's activities.[32] According to Meiklejohn, political speech is essential for self-government.

For example, according to the self-government argument, anything said during a political debate would be protected. But a paid lobbyist's words and actions would be limited under this model, because he or she is acting for a personal reason. The political debate is benefiting society. The lobbyist's actions are only benefiting a small number of people.

*Court case: **New York Times** v. **Sullivan** (1964).* A new standard was set by the Supreme Court, making it difficult for public officials to prove libel. The police commissioner of Montgomery, Alabama, L. B. Sullivan, sued *The New York Times* because he said that a full-page ad in support of the civil rights movement contained misleading and false information about him.[33] The ad criticized the conduct of the police at a civil rights demonstration. Some of the statements in the ad were false. For instance, it said that police had "ringed the Alabama State College campus" where a civil rights demonstration took place, while in reality, they massed on one side of the campus; and it said that Dr. Martin Luther King, Jr., had been arrested seven times, while he had actually been arrested four times. Because the *Times* did

This civil rights demonstration was held in Washington, D.C., in 1963. A newspaper ad supporting civil rights efforts led to the groundbreaking case of New York Times v. Sullivan.

not verify all statements in the ad, Sullivan won $500,000 in damages from an Alabama court. The Supreme Court overturned that ruling; Sullivan could not prove that the ad was about him, because he was not named, nor could he prove the *Times* knew the statements were false. A public official cannot seek damages for a defamation unless he proves it was said with actual malice (knowledge of falsity or reckless disregard for the truth). Sullivan could not prove actual malice. The Supreme Court established that the press has protection if it prints criticism of government or its officials, and this standard for libel was later applied to public figures as well. Everyone, papers included, makes mistakes. In this case, the mistakes were minor, and no real damage was done to Sullivan's reputation.

The Safety-Valve Argument

A fifth argument, the "safety valve," was—like the self-fulfillment argument—proposed by Thomas I. Emerson of Yale University. This argument claims that people are more open to ideas once they have discussed them. Proponents of this argument feel that free expression and the ability to talk about controversies lessen the chance of controversial issues escalating into violence.[34] Citizens voice their opinions about any topic, and this acts as a safety valve for society by allowing all opinions to be heard.[35] Proponents of the safety-valve argument feel that citizens participate more in government when their ideas are discussed and that government is more responsive to citizens when all opinions are voiced.

For example, a discussion of school regulations is held at a school board meeting. You feel some of the regulations go too far. As a student, you are allowed to speak your opinion.

Court case: **Whitney** *v.* **California** *(1927).* Anita Whitney was convicted of violating the California Criminal Syndicalism Act because she was an active member in the Communist Labor Party. Although her conviction was upheld by the Supreme Court, Justices Holmes and Louis Brandeis urged the adoption of the clear and present danger rule. Justice Brandeis warned, "It is hazardous to discourage thought, hope and imagination . . ."[36]

The Tolerance Argument

A final argument for freedom of speech is tolerance. Dean Lee Bollinger wrote in 1986 that freedom of speech should "help shape the intellectual character of society" in *The Tolerant Society: Freedom of Speech and Extremist Speech in America*.[37] Supporters of this argument believe when people put up with speech that they do not agree with, they practice tolerance, which has a positive effect on society: namely, allowing pure freedom of speech.[38]

If someone does not like what is being done or said, he or she can ignore it. People are capable of free choice and they can choose to ignore inciteful or hateful words or actions, according to proponents of tolerance.

For example, if someone at school calls you an insulting name, you can ignore that person and deny them what they are after: a reaction.

Court case: **Skokie, Village of *v*. National Socialist Party of America** *(1978)*. When members of the National Socialist Party of America (NSPA), a neo-Nazi group, wanted to demonstrate in Skokie, a predominantly Jewish suburb of Chicago, the village could not prevent it. They were forced to practice tolerance. Skokie's population was roughly half Jewish. Approximately five thousand people there were survivors of Adolf Hitler's concentration camps. They passed ordinances to keep the Nazis out of Skokie, but those ordinances were ruled unconstitutional by the U.S. District Court. The court held that Skokie could not stop the Nazi group from marching. In turn, the Nazis could not antagonize the village. The wearing of Nazi uniforms and the use of swastikas was protected as freedom of expression. The Illinois Supreme Court decided that not allowing the NSPA to demonstrate would equal prior restraint.

The Holocaust survivors practiced tolerance. Many were terrified at what the Nazi group represented. The survivors had past experiences of abuse during the Holocaust. Most had lost family members in concentration camps. The thought of the National Socialist Party of America holding a rally in their community triggered anxiety and emotional trauma to Skokie residents. Illinois Supreme Court judges knew this but decided to let the Nazis speak their hatred against Jews. Their reasoning? There was no captive audience. By allowing the NSPA to speak, society remains committed to free speech.[39] It was protection against more groups like the NSPA forming.[40] If America could tolerate groups like the NSPA, who advocate hate through their doctrines, then American society is protected against Nazism because by allowing all speech, even hate speech, Americans decide for themselves what to say, do, and think.

In the end, the NSPA never did march in Skokie. They marched at Federal Building Plaza and later at Marquette Park, Chicago, with counterdemonstrations against them.[41]

This chapter focused on some of the major arguments that support freedom of speech. In the next chapter, arguments for limiting freedom of speech will be investigated.

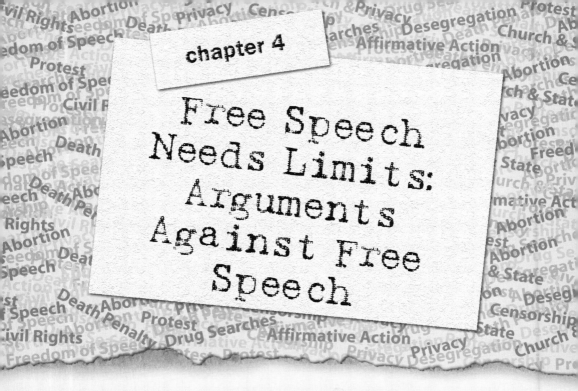

chapter 4

Free Speech Needs Limits: Arguments Against Free Speech

Opponents of free speech propose a number of different arguments supporting their position. Although most in our society would agree that freedom of speech is a right, some feel that allowing pure free speech restricts other freedoms. While critics of pure free speech believe in reasonable limits,[1] who sets those limits makes a big difference. Sometimes those who want regulation of rights only want other people's rights restricted, not their own.[2]

Objections to the Marketplace Argument

Critics of the marketplace argument question whether the give and take of the marketplace will produce the right decision. Whose truth is considered the standard? In any discussion or argument, there are at least two sides. People are not always rational during disagreements, and each person sees truth differently. Each side uses words, or speech, to sway the opposing side. No speech is totally free from politics or ideology. Some believe the idea valued by the majority, whether true or false, is the highest value.[3] For critics of the marketplace argument, free speech is a listener's right to hear or not to hear something, not a speaker's right to say something.[4]

Critics of free speech ask: Can society afford the delay the marketplace requires? Time is necessary for an idea to prove itself or fade away. For example, genocide may be challenged by free speech or may be endorsed by free speech. In the marketplace, genocide may prove to be unjust and wrong. But while society is waiting, how many people are murdered? Think about Hitler's concentration camps. Millions of people were murdered as Hitler exercised his right to speak hate. Many of those murdered did not have the chance to speak their opinions. Critics of free speech would say that the marketplace of ideas failed those who were killed.

Court case: **Wisconsin** *v.* **Mitchell** *(1993).* A black youth, Todd Mitchell, was convicted of inciting other African Americans to attack a white youth; two years were added to his sentence because the crime was motivated by racial hatred.[5] He chose the victim because of his race. If the marketplace argument holds up, the black youth's comments would not be punished. Ultimately, the "right" decision would be made by those listening to Mitchell. Instead, a group of black men and boys attacked a white youth, severely beating him, merely because of his race.[6]

Objections to the Worthwhile-Speech Argument

When dealing with Chafee's worthwhile versus worthless speech argument, critics ask: How does a person define the two sides? What one person views as worthwhile individual speech may not be worthwhile to someone else. One person might find certain words offensive. Someone else might not.

For example, a classmate in your school might find the terms "gay" or "stupid" offensive. Other students in your school might not take offense at those words. Whose side is worthwhile, and whose is worthless?

Court case: **United States *v.* O'Brien** *(1968).* David O'Brien burned his draft card, in violation of a 1965 amendment to the Selective Service Act. O'Brien said his act was a symbolic protest of the Vietnam War and the law violated his First Amendment rights.[7] The Supreme Court disagreed, saying that the 1965 amendment served a legitimate governmental interest, more important than his individual freedom of speech.[8] This case put limits on freedom of expression, which many people feel is a key component to freedom of speech. This case also initiated a new test to determine whether expression, or nonspeech, should be protected. Expression is not protected if it interferes with government interest. Burning the draft card interfered with the Selective Service doing its job. There are limits on the conduct that someone can engage in while making a free speech statement. When both speech and nonspeech elements are combined to make a statement, sometimes the nonspeech element is not protected as a First Amendment right. Each case is different, and some forms of symbolic speech do qualify for First Amendment protection.

Applying Chafee's worthwhile/worthless-speech argument to the O'Brien case, the symbolic speech of burning a draft card was determined to be worthless in terms of First Amendment protection. O'Brien had every right to protest the Vietnam War and could have done so through speech. Had he given a speech against the war, he would have had full protection. Because he chose to burn his draft card, he interfered with the maintenance and integrity of the Selective Service, which was a government interest. That symbolic action moved his speech from protected to unprotected.

Objections to the Self-Government Argument

The most effective argument against Meiklejohn's self-government argument is that it protects political speech but not nonpolitical speech, which is a very narrow definition of protected speech. The line between the two is blurry. Almost all speech contains private emotions. Who decides the difference? Even Supreme Court justices have political opinions, which are reflected in each justice's decision. Not all individuals have the time or interest to participate in politics, which is necessary for self-government. Meiklejohn's definition is narrow in scope. He believes everything worth saying should be said, but that not everyone should speak—only those whose message is politically worthy.[9]

For example: Two people live in your town. One is well educated and has time to devote to politics. The other is not well educated and has no time for politics. Under the self-government argument for free speech, would both of these people be allowed to speak their opinions?

Court case: **Debs** *v.* **United States** *(1919).* Eugene Debs was convicted of pamphleteering under the 1917 Espionage Act, not because of advocacy but because of the tendency of his antiwar speeches to encourage men to ignore the draft. The Supreme Court upheld his conviction, saying that he intended to interfere with the draft.[10] Under

Meiklejohn's self-government argument, Debs should have been allowed to speak his opinion, since it was political speech.

Objections to the Safety-Valve Argument

Critics of the safety-valve argument believe that too much discussion can lead to violence.

For example, suppose a controversial issue in your school is whether or not boys should be allowed to wear skirts. Opponents of the safety-valve argument would say that too much discussion of this issue would lead to fistfights among the boys.

*Court case: **FCC** v. **Pacifica Foundation** (1978)*. George Carlin, a satiric humorist, had a twelve-minute monologue entitled "Filthy Words" that was broadcast over the radio at two o'clock in the after-noon. The Supreme Court upheld the FCC's authority to limit broadcasts containing indecent words to late-night hours, where children would make up very little of the audience.[11] Those opposed to the safety-valve argument point to this case. If this argument were valid, there would be no decisions such as in this case. All words could be spoken at any time to any audience.

Objections to the Tolerance Argument

Many take offense at what the tolerance argument seems to protect. Why should a person tolerate hateful acts or words? Does this model advocate hate? Regardless of what we were told as young children, words do hurt, especially when words and actions are linked.

Let's return to the Skokie march. Why did the Jewish community have to tolerate a racist, hateful march by a group of people who chose Skokie because it was Jewish? Many people do not understand this ruling. Had the group asked to march on a street in Chicago, it would have been a different situation. There might have been Jews and Holocaust survivors in the audience, but the bulk of the citizens of Chicago are not Jewish or survivors of concentration camps. A group of Holocaust survivors pleaded that the National Socialist Party of America not be allowed to march because of the imminent harm that march would cause to the survivors.[12]

Many felt the derogatory remarks made directly at the Jews in order to intimidate them had the potential to cause enough psychological harm to warrant an exception to First Amendment protection for the NSPA.[13] What the Court eventually decided was that it was allowable because no one was required to pay attention to it. Unless a captive audience is forced to listen to something, people do not have the constitutional right to not be insulted.

Negative consequences of this forced tolerance include emotional trauma, the risk of violence because Skokie's "turf" is invaded by a dangerous "enemy," and the courts giving subtle respectability to a group like the NSPA by allowing them to march in a Jewish community. What Skokie feared was that hate groups like the NSPA would gain legitimacy that would lead to a breakdown of the community, which happened in Europe when Hitler preached his message of anti-Semitism.[14]

Because the NSPA was a political group, it was given full First Amendment protection, regardless of its message.

Critics of the outcome of the Skokie case point out that racial insults can cause long-term harm.[15]

When a neo-Nazi group wanted to march in Skokie, Illinois, an area with a large Jewish population, the group's First Amendment rights were upheld despite their offensive opinions.

These critics view words as weapons and feel that only the victims of racial insults can determine whether or not they are harmful. They feel the courts have set a dangerous precedent.[16]

Court case: **Bethel School District** *v.* **Fraser** *(1986).* A graduating senior at Bethel High School delivered a nominating speech for a classmate at a school-sponsored assembly. The speech was vulgar, containing sexual references, and embarrassed many students and faculty.

The student was suspended. Rather than accept the tolerance argument, school officials punished the student for his speech, and acted to protect other students from indecent speech. The Supreme Court ruled that the school was right to discipline the student because his speech was inappropriate and lewd and was given in a public school setting.[17] He was a student, not an adult, and the listeners were considered a captive audience.[18] Had he said the same things walking between classes, it would have been a different story. Maintaining an orderly atmosphere conducive to education is more important than one student's right to free speech, according to the Court.[19]

Critics do not believe that pure freedom of speech is a good thing or that it should be allowed in this society. They believe some limits are necessary to provide a safe environment for all people. Some believe in a "greater good" argument—that individual's rights are less important than the needs of society. In other words, sometimes individuals must make sacrifices in order to ensure that society functions in ways to protect all individuals. Safety of citizens and national security are more important than broad liberty. They are willing to give up some personal freedoms in order to make our country a safe land.

A student at your school talks about killing all persons of Middle Eastern descent because of the World Trade Center attacks on September 11, 2001. He justifies his views by saying that most terrorists come from Middle Eastern countries. Does this student's right to free speech mean he can advocate murder?

Court case: **State of Montana** *v.* **Robinson** *(2003).* Malachi Robinson tried to goad a police officer into a fight by cursing at him at a stoplight. The Montana Supreme Court ruled that a person cannot randomly curse at police officers, even though officers are trained to keep cool under those circumstances. The justices ruled that any obscene language likely to provoke a fight can result in a disorderly conduct charge. Robinson's swearing was not protected by the First Amendment.[20] The judges determined that he used fighting words, which are not protected.

This chapter focused on the arguments against free speech. Next we will look at laws concerning the issue.

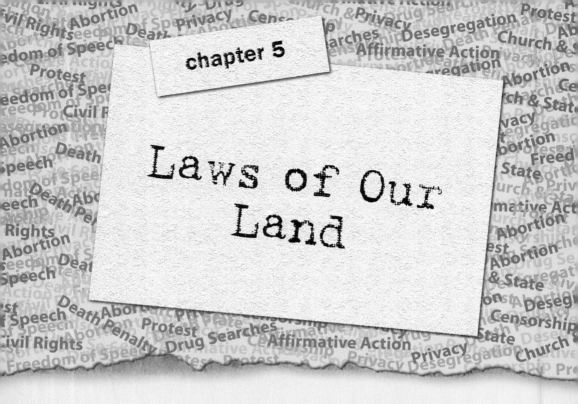

chapter 5

Laws of Our Land

When the Bill of Rights was ratified in 1791, the First Amendment guaranteed all citizens the right to free speech. What was intended by this amendment? All forms of expression or only speech? In the beginning, like the Greeks, the United States granted freedom of expression only to elite males, excluding women, slaves, and aliens from exercising free speech.[1]

The Alien and Sedition Acts

In 1798, the Alien and Sedition Acts were passed. They were four separate acts but are generally talked about together. The Naturalization Act required immigrants to reside in America fourteen years before becoming citizens. (Previously, it had been five years.) The Alien Act and the Alien

Enemies Act allowed the president to detain or expel any alien he suspected of spying. The Sedition Act punished any writing against the government.[2] These four acts resulted from foreign policy disputes with France. Most French citizens living in America were openly critical of President John Adams, a member of the Federalist Party. The Federalists believed that patriotism meant to agree with the government, and anyone who disagreed was committing sedition.[3] The Alien and Sedition Acts served as revenge.[4]

The Sedition Act was enforced more stringently than the Alien Acts. As Michael Kent Curtis explains in *Free Speech, "The People's Darling Privilege,"* although no license was needed to publish anything, if a press published something that was considered "dangerous or offensive writings," the publisher could face punishment under the Sedition Act.[5]

Most of the convictions under these acts were of members of the other major political party, the Democratic-Republicans. This party, known as the Republicans (though it is distinct from today's Republican party), was organized by Thomas Jefferson to oppose the extension of slavery. Federalists opposed the Republicans because they wanted to maintain control of the country.[6] For instance, Matthew Lyon, a Republican congressman from Vermont, served a four-month prison sentence for criticizing President Adams. Insisting that his statements were true, he challenged the constitutionality of the Sedition Act.

In 1801, Thomas Jefferson (a Democratic-Republican) became president and pardoned those who had been convicted, calling the acts unconstitutional. He wrote resolutions that allowed Virginia and Kentucky to accuse the federal government of

Legal Terms

appellate court (also called court of appeals)—A court that reviews decisions of lower courts for fairness and accuracy. An appellate court can reverse a lower court's ruling.

appellant or petitioner—The person who feels the lower court made an error.

appellee or respondent—The person who won the case in the lower court.

brief—Written statement of a party's argument on one or more issues in the case.

majority opinion—The ruling and reasoning supported by a majority of appellate court judges in a case. **Concurring opinions** are written by judges who agree with the majority opinion but have other reasons for their views. **Dissenting opinions** are written by judges who disagree with the ruling.

precedent—A legal holding that will determine how courts decide future cases.

exceeding its powers. The acts expired in 1801. Many of today's experts on the First Amendment agree with Jefferson: The acts were unconstitutional and only passed to silence newspapers and individuals critical of Adams.[7]

The Espionage Act

During World War I, Congress passed the Espionage Act of 1917, prohibiting criticism of the war. To prevent sabotage and communication of military secrets to the enemy, it was a crime to "willfully utter, print, write, or publish any disloyal, profane, scurrilous, or abusive language" about the United States. Any speech that interfered with military operation, promoted enemy success, attempted to cause mutiny or refusal of duty in the armed forces, or interfered with the draft was punishable with up to twenty years in prison or a fine of $10,000.[8] More than two thousand people were convicted of violating the Espionage Act. For the first time, the Supreme Court ruled on the issue of free speech.[9] Charles Schenck was convicted under this law for distributing antidraft pamphlets during World War I. This was the landmark case in which clear and present danger was first announced. This test stated that words used in circumstances that create a clear and present danger are not protected by the First Amendment.

Also in 1917, Congress made it illegal to

threaten the life of the president of the United States. The law has been amended to include all officers in order of succession to the president, and it has been upheld as constitutional. Making a threat to the president is not protected speech under the First Amendment.

Laws Against Anarchism and Communism

Following World War I, states without existing anti-syndicalism laws passed them to battle what they saw as union danger. Syndicalism is a movement that promoted the idea that production should be for the good of society, not for profit. It promotes anarchy (absence of government). By 1925, two thirds of states had these laws. These state laws punished at state levels what the Alien and Sedition Acts punished at national levels.

The Smith Act of 1940 punished speech that tried to create disloyalty in the military, advocated overthrowing the government, or conspired to violate the act. The law allowed seizure of printed material that violated the act, and it provided a maximum fine of $10,000 and ten years in prison. These penalties were later doubled.[10]

During this period, there was strong anti-Communism hysteria, and Americans who joined the Communist Party found their lives forever changed by that association. In 1951, American citizens Eugene Dennis and ten other members of the Central Committee of the Communist Party were indicted under the Smith Act for advocating the overthrow of the United States. They did not attempt an overthrow; they wanted one and talked about a future time when it could be achieved. They wanted the American government to fail. In *Dennis* v. *United States* (1951), the Supreme Court upheld the Smith Act. Even though a clear and present danger was not demonstrated, the convictions stood because it was believed Communism was a great enough evil. The conspiracy was punished in order to avoid possible violent revolution. According to the Supreme Court, the government did not have to wait until a revolution began; the United States had the right to prevent revolution.

However, a few years later, in *Yates* v. *United States* (1957), the Court decided that the specific advocacy of violent overthrow was required, not simply the abstract idea of revolution. Oleta Yates and thirteen members of the Communist Party had discussed the necessity of a violent overthrow but did not plan one. They were convicted under the Smith Act in federal court. The Supreme Court ruled that abstract doctrine (the advocacy of ideas permitted in the Smith Act) was legal. The case was remanded (sent back) to the district court for retrial and acquittal. No new cases have been tried under the Smith Act because of the difficulty of proving the difference between idea and advocacy. The advocacy of violent retribution, which is an unlawful action, may be punished.

Laws Against Draft Resistance

The Selective Service Act of 1948 made it illegal to advise those eligible for the draft to resist conscription. A Kansas physician told his stepson not to register. He was convicted in 1949 and sent to prison. In 1950, the dean of men at a Mennonite college urged students not to register. He was convicted. During the Vietnam War of the 1960s, Dr. Benjamin Spock and the Reverend William Sloan Coffin were convicted of unlawfully counseling draft-age men to refuse or evade military service. The convictions were overturned. Until the Supreme Court rules definitively on this issue, advocating draft evasion is expression not protected by the First Amendment.

The Freedom of Information Act

The Freedom of Information Act (FOIA) was passed in 1966, allowing any person limited access to certain records of the executive branch of government. This was done to encourage disclosure between the government and its people. The FOIA applies only to federal agencies. It provides access to records that already exist and does not require the government to research and create a new record. Any person—members of the press, foreign nationals, corporations, university researchers, members of the state and local governments, and private citizens—is permitted to request records. In order for the public to be fully informed of government actions, the public needs to have access to government records. Only then can the public make informed decisions and participate fully in government.

Not every government agency is accessible under the FOIA. Some records are kept secret in the interest of national security. Both the CIA and FBI are allowed to withhold records. Law enforcement manuals, confidential financial information, private information about government employees (such as marital status, medical problems, and religious preferences), trial records, audits, and oil well information are a few of the records that can be withheld.

The Sunshine Act was passed in 1976, requiring an open-meeting policy for various agencies within the executive branch, for similar reasons that the FOIA was passed. Exemptions similar to those for the FOIA apply to the Sunshine Act as well. Journalists use both the FOIA and the Sunshine Act to gain access to important news, and they pass that news on to the general public.

Eugene V. Debs was president of the Socialist Party. The Socialists spoke out against America's participation in World War I, urging young men to resist the draft. The Supreme Court upheld the right of the government to limit this kind of speech if it posed a "clear and present danger."

Laws on Intelligence

The Intelligence Identities Protection Act of 1982 makes it a crime to publish identities of secret agents for the United States. Countries around the world are interested in learning who our spies are. In 1975, Richard S. Welch was murdered in front of his home in Greece. He was the CIA Station Chief in Athens, and his identity had been publicized a month before his murder. In 1980, a few hours after an official of the American Embassy in Kingston, Jamaica, was identified, he was almost assassinated. These and other incidents contributed to the passage of this act.[11]

On October 7, 2004, Judith Miller, a reporter for *The New York Times*, was jailed because she refused to answer questions to a grand jury that was investigating who had told reporters about a CIA official's identity. Miller believed she had the right to refuse to answer questions to protect her sources. Judge Thomas Hogan ruled that reporters must answer questions from a grand jury when relating to matters concerning national security. Other journalists testified to the grand jury, some with their sources' approval.[12]

In 1993, Congress amended the Hatch Act of 1939. The original act limited the political activities of civil service employees of the executive branch. They could join political parties, discuss their views in private, and vote, but they could not distribute campaign material, organize or manage political rallies, or make campaign speeches in partisan elections. The amendment to the Hatch Act allows federal workers to campaign outside the workplace and to hold office in political party organizations.

Laws on Broadcasting and the Internet

The Cable Act of 1992 allowed cable television operators to decide whether to transmit indecent programming. While obscenity is banned from transmission, indecent programs that are not obscene may be shown at operators' discretion.[13] Because there are fewer restrictions on cable channels than on networks, many feel that cable operators are pushing the boundaries of good taste and decency by showing certain programs with nudity, sexual content, and objectionable language.[14]

The Communications Decency Act (CDA) was passed in 1996 to ban the transmission of obscene or indecent material across the Internet. Cathleen Cleaver, director of legal studies at the Family Research Council, a conservative organization, argued that in the real world, obscene material was not legally allowed in places where there are children. But in cyberspace, children can gain access to Web sites that promote pornography and display obscene images. Other supporters of the law said it was impossible for parents to monitor their children when they are at libraries, schools, and other places where Internet access is available.[15] The CDA proposed standards to regulate the Internet using broadcast media rules rather than the looser standards of print media. Minors cannot escape broadcast media as easily as they can ignore material in print.[16] The CDA also prohibited transmitting obscene or indecent messages to minors.[17]

In 1997, the CDA was ruled unconstitutional for being too broad and vague. In free speech issues, if a law is ruled to be too broad, it means that the definition of the law punishes speech that is constitutionally protected as well as speech that is not protected. If a law is ruled to be too vague, it means that people have to guess at its meaning and its application to speech. Law must be narrowly drawn and specifically defined so that speakers know what is and what is not protected by the First Amendment. The rationale is that society may be harmed either by underprotecting speech or over-protecting it.[18] According to the Supreme Court, the CDA restricted adults from sending and receiving messages they had a right to view.[19] The Court said that freedom of expression outweighs vague censorship, even when the intention of the law is to protect minors.[20]

Many feared that in order to protect minors from obscenity or indecency, adults would be denied access to the same materials.[21] Opponents of the CDA feel that blocking software and parental supervision provide all the necessary safety that children need to utilize the Internet. They also point to existing laws that already ban obscenity and child pornography.[22] As stated by Justice John Paul Stevens in *Reno* v. *ACLU* (1997), "The Internet receives full protection of the First Amendment."[23] To protect anonymous communication online and the right to communicate in private without fear of being overhead by others, Congress passed the Electronic Communications Privacy Act in 1986.[24] The Internet is a relatively new medium, and law related to it will be continually changing for years to come.

The USA PATRIOT Act

The USA PATRIOT Act—which stands for **U**niting and **S**trengthening **A**merica by **P**roviding **A**ppropriate **T**ools **R**equired to **I**ntercept and **O**bstruct **T**errorism—was passed on October 26, 2001, six weeks after the terrorist attacks on the World Trade Center and the Pentagon. It allows the FBI to obtain records through secret court orders, as well as track and eavesdrop on e-mail and telephone communications.[25]

There has been a great deal of argument about the act. One side is in favor of relinquishing some personal freedom to protect national security, especially since terrorism has occurred on American soil. If a person is doing nothing wrong, added surveillance should not matter and he or she should not object to it, say supporters of the Patriot Act.

People on the other side feel that giving up any personal freedom is giving up too much. Those opposed to this act believe it is just the first freedom Americans will be giving up. They warn that other restrictions will follow, for the sake of safety. Even though they are doing nothing wrong, they do not want their communications or activities monitored, even if it means risking another terrorist attack.

On June 5, 2003, Attorney General John Ashcroft asked Congress to expand the Patriot Act. Some in Congress want to limit the law, but Ashcroft believes the law has weaknesses that need to be fixed. Several changes are proposed, including denying material on suspected terrorists in government custody to be released through the FOIA; a DNA database on suspected terrorists; pretrial detention for suspected terrorists; and expatriating American citizens who support terrorist organizations. Critics worry that free speech will be eroded by those changes and want to limit the expansion of government power.

"Our ability to prevent another catastrophic attack on American soil would be more difficult if not impossible without the Patriot Act," Ashcroft told the House Judiciary Committee.[26] He also has said,

> If we knew then what we know now, we would have passed the Patriot Act six months before Sept. 11

rather than six weeks after the attacks. The cause we have chosen is just. The course we have chosen is constitutional.[27]

Critics of the Patriot Act, including the American Civil Liberties Union (ACLU) and the American Library Association, are concerned about free speech limits included in the act. Particularly troubling are sections 206, 214, 215, and 216. Section 206 permits "roving wiretaps" and secret court orders to monitor electronic communications to investigate terrorists. Sections 214 and 216 extend telephone monitoring authority, including routing and addressing information for Internet traffic. Section 215 grants the FBI and other law enforcement agencies the power to obtain search warrants for business, medical, educational, library, and bookstore records that they feel are related to any terrorism investigation.[28] People feel they can be targeted for their beliefs because of the increased government surveillance power. Also, librarians cannot tell patrons if their records have been investigated. Many of them feel the gag order is unjust.

On September 30, 2004, federal judge Victor Marrero ruled that a component of the Patriot Act was unconstitutional. The FBI could demand information from Internet service providers without any judicial oversight or public review. He ruled that the law, as written, was overbroad.[29]

chapter 6

According to the Courts

Countless court cases have shaped the issue of free speech. As Raoul Berger states in *Congress v. The Supreme Court*, when the Constitution was drafted, those men believed that the Supreme Court had the right to judicial review, setting up the system we have today, in which the Supreme Court has the final say in a court decision.[1] Most of the definitive court cases about freedom of speech have been decided by the Supreme Court. Let's look at a few cases whose outcomes significantly changed the country's definition or acceptance of freedom of speech.

***Texas* v. *Johnson* (1989).** Gregory Lee Johnson burned an American flag, claiming political protest. He felt he was being forced to be patriotic, and he believed the United States was a country of aggression.[2] Convicted of flag desecration under a Texas law, he appealed to the Supreme Court. They overturned that conviction, saying that his action was protected under the First Amendment. This ruling touched off an intense, emotional national debate.[3]

Many people do not understand this ruling. If burning the flag does not count as desecration, they ask, what does? Even the Supreme Court justices disagreed on this subject, voting 5–4. Justice Anthony M. Kennedy voted with the majority, but he did not want to. As he said, "the flag protects those who hold it in contempt." His decision was a tough one. He felt that although he disliked voting for overturning the conviction, Johnson's flag burning was speech and the Constitution demanded that his action be protected.[4] Justice William J. Brennan, Jr., voted against the Texas law, saying that it was unconstitutional because it punished political speech that might be offensive.

The justices who dissented believed that the flag was a symbol of the fight for liberty and equality and should be protected from destruction when the acts that destroy it are used to antagonize others. Justice William H. Rehnquist equated Johnson's action to fighting words, which are not protected.[5] Justice John Paul Stevens disagreed with the majority, believing that the flag was protected from desecration. He was a World War II veteran and was offended by the action of Johnson. In his opinion, if the flag was worth fighting for in a war, then it should have protection. He felt that the flag was a unique symbol[6] that was exempt from laws.

The flag is a symbol of our country, and we are taught from an early age to show respect by pledging our allegiance to it, by placing our hands over our hearts when it is presented at sporting events,

In 1989, the Supreme Court held that flag burning was a protected form of expression. This caused national debate and a call for a constitutional amendment to forbid desecrating the flag.

and by ensuring the flag does not touch the ground. Some people, to show their frustration and disagreement with the government, choose to burn the flag in protest. Because of protests against the Vietnam War that involved destroying American flags, by 1971, every state had statutes that forbade defacing or showing disrespect for the American flag.[7] Chief Justice Rehnquist included the flag's history in their dissensions. Those state laws have been used to prosecute people. Supporters of such statutes want to know the definition of desecration. To them, flag burning, spitting, and calling the symbol of America a rag means flag desecration, regardless of the reason for such expression. For the justices, the meaning of a person's action determines whether or not he or she is desecrating the flag. If he or she is burning a flag during a political protest, it is protected speech. If he or she drags the flag through the mud without stating any message, it is desecration and not protected action.

After the *Johnson* ruling, the American public was outraged. To many, the ruling said it was OK to burn the flag. There were counterprotests by those who supported a constitutional amendment punishing any desecration of the flag.[8] The amendment issue faded, but the case shows how expression with a strong emotional component causes debate within society and within the court chambers. It also showed that symbolic speech is protected, even when justices disagree with the actions, and because this case had a small majority, the issue might come up again.

Roth v. **United States** *(1957)*. Samuel Roth violated the Comstock Act of 1873 by mailing advertisements for his pornographic publications. The Comstock Act banned works that were considered indecent, including those that contained anything to do with birth control or abortion. Some of the works banned by this act include *For Whom the Bell Tolls* by Ernest Hemingway, *Ulysses* by James Joyce, and *All Quiet on the Western Front* by Erich Maria Remarque. The Supreme Court has interpreted the Comstock Act over the years to better define obscenity, and the act is still part of federal law. The Court determined that the obscenity provisions in this act were constitutional and defined obscenity as worthless and sexually lewd acts or speech.[9] (Lewd acts or speech are those that intend to excite lust or sexual desire in a way that is offensive to the average person.) As Justice Brennan said, "Implicit in the history of the First Amendment is the rejection of obscenity as utterly without redeeming social importance." Because obscenity adds nothing of value to society, the Court said, it is not protected speech.[10] One problem in this ruling is that the definition of obscenity is overly vague.[11]

***Ginsberg* v. *New York* (1968).** This case determined that the target audience of material can determine whether something is considered obscene. Something not considered obscene when seen or read by adults can be obscene if targeted to minors, or if minors even see the material. Sam Ginsberg was convicted of violating New York law that prohibited the selling of harmful material to minors because a sixteen-year-old boy bought a girlie magazine from Ginsberg's store. Selling the same magazine to an adult did not break any law.

***Chaplinsky* v. *New Hampshire* (1942).** When Walter Chaplinsky was arrested, he called the arresting officer a fascist. (Fascism is a type of dictatorship.) He cursed and used derogatory language, and he was convicted for using foul language and fighting words. The Court divides expression into worthwhile versus worthless. Worthless expression includes fighting words as well as words that are lewd, obscene, profane, or libelous. These types of speech are of such low value that they have no worthwhile place in society.[12] The Court decided that words that inflict injury upon the listener and incite an immediate breach of the peace are fighting words. The Court's definition referred to the "average" person. But there is disagreement over who is considered average and who should determine it.[13] Since it is difficult to define average, this definition was unclear in the courts.

Fighting words can be different for each person or groups of people. However, the Court ruled that because Chaplinsky used language that would normally provoke someone into a violent reaction, his speech was not protected by the First Amendment.

Tinker v. ***Des Moines Independent Community School District*** *(1969).* Students Mary Beth Tinker, John Tinker, and Christopher Eckhardt wore black armbands to protest the Vietnam War, violating a school policy against such expression. They were suspended. A lower court ruled that a school ban on armbands was constitutional and, although sympathetic to the students, ruled against them. The Supreme Court overturned that judgment and ruled in their favor, saying that the armbands were a form of symbolic expression[14] and that the students were exercising their First Amendment rights.[15] The school district could not prove that by wearing the armbands, the students interfered with school activities or lessons. The armbands did not interfere with the rights of other students. The action did not result in disciplinary problems, because the armbands were silent and passive. The Court held that elementary and secondary students had free speech rights, but not the freedom to cause riots or be disruptive. Students can express their views in nonthreatening ways.

R.A.V. v. **St. Paul** (1992). Three skinhead youths burned a cross on the front lawn of an African-American family who had moved into a white neighborhood in Minnesota. The teenagers could have been charged with one of many other crimes, including terroristic threats, arson, or criminal damage to property. The prosecution in the case chose to use the Bias-Motivated Crime Ordinance to charge the youths rather than the other laws. The Supreme Court ruled that expressive conduct was protected, regardless of the message. The Court was split on this case. The majority opinion held that if this type of expression counted as fighting words and so was forbidden, then all fighting words would have to be covered so broadly that all free expression would be curbed.[16] The dissenting justices felt that this allowed hate speech and implied that intimidation was acceptable expression.[17] They pointed out the difference between speech that does not harm someone and speech that does. This case illustrates both hate speech and hateful acts and the dilemma judges face when deciding whose rights are more important.

People v. **Bruce** (1964). Lenny Bruce was a stand-up comic who performed in adult clubs. He used terms that were considered obscene, and he included gestures in his comedy acts that many people found obscene. Lenny Bruce's case never went to the Supreme Court. However, it was important because the Illinois Supreme Court overturned his convictions of violating obscenity laws because Bruce was using satire in his comedy act. Though the judges did not necessarily approve of his choice of words or acts, they felt there was some redeeming social importance to his routine.[18]

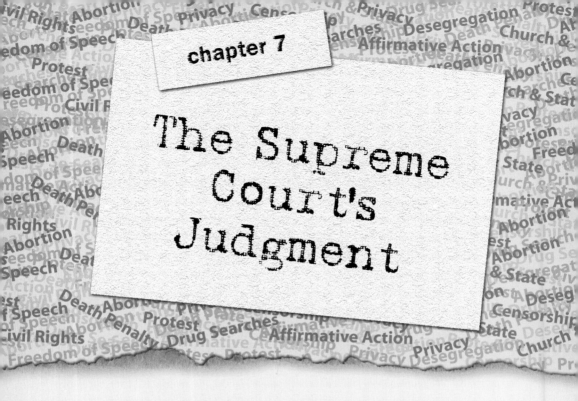

chapter 7

The Supreme Court's Judgment

The Supreme Court, made up of nine justices, is our country's highest court. It is assumed that the framers of the Constitution expected the Supreme Court to make judgments in cases in which no clear right or wrong could easily be determined.[1] The following Supreme Court cases have determined precedents (legal decisions that serve as examples or justifications for later rulings). Some restricted rights of private citizens in order to protect the safety of the country. These cases have defined the role of free speech in our society.

Schenck v. United States

The Selective Service Act of World War I was passed in May 1917 and provided for the registration of all men ages twenty-one through thirty to serve in the United States armed forces. The system provided manpower for war production as well as soldiers, and it exempted government officials and clergymen. Conscientious objectors were excused from combat duty. The reason for enacting the Selective Service Act was to ensure America had enough men to fight in the war.

Prior to World War I, the United States relied on volunteers, based on the colonial tradition of the militia, where able-bodied men trained with militia units and fought with them during battles. Sometimes states had to resort to drafting men into the militias when America had too few men to fight. During the Civil War, every citizen was encouraged to defend the nation. The Draft Act of 1863, sometimes called the Enrollment Act, established the federal government's right to call citizens to service rather than rely on state action.

During World War I, there was strong opposition to the draft. Those opposed expressed their feelings in different ways: marches, burning draft cards, and burning American flags. Charles Schenck, a member of the Socialist Party, opposed the draft and United States entry into the war. Socialism stands for state ownership and control of the means of production and distribution of wealth. Socialists urge reconstruction of capitalist political systems through peaceful, democratic, and parliamentary means. The Socialist Party denounced World War I.

Schenck circulated pamphlets encouraging men to avoid conscription and mailed them to draftees. He compared draftees to convicts and slaves, implying that the government was violating laws.[2] He was convicted under the Espionage Act of 1917 because his speech was tied to an action intended to interfere with the draft. The Espionage Act was aimed at those who interfered with American involvement in the war. The clear and present danger test was announced with this case; someone has to show real danger before he can be convicted. In this case, the danger was in Schenck's urging to evade the draft. The words Schenck used in his leaflets created a clear and present danger; he was trying to interfere with the government's carrying out of the draft.[3]

This was a landmark case because speech was tied to action that posed a clear and present danger. Speech must create a significant, real risk of an evil that is against the law, and the speech must be tied to an action that will lead to the evil, said the Court.[4] However, the Court rarely used the doctrine of clear and present danger to strike down laws under the First Amendment over the ensuing years, and other tests were established to further define what was protected and what was not.

Excerpts from the Socialist Party Pamphlet

ASSERT YOUR RIGHTS!

If you do not assert and support your rights, you are helping to "deny or disparage rights" which it is the solemn duty of all citizens and residents of the United States to retain. . . .

In lending . . . silent consent to the conscription law, in neglecting to assert your rights, you are . . . helping to condone and support a most infamous and insidious conspiracy to abridge and destroy the sacred and cherished rights of a free people. You are a citizen: not a subject! . . .

No power was delegated to send our citizens away to foreign shores to shoot up the people of other lands, no matter what may be their internal or international disputes. . .

To draw this country into the horrors of the present war in Europe, to force the youth of our land into the shambles and bloody trenches of war-crazy nations, would be a crime the magnitude of which defies description. . . .

You are responsible. You must do your share to maintain, support, and uphold the rights of the people of this country.

In this world crisis where do you stand? Are you with the forces of liberty and light or war and darkness?

Exercise your rights of free speech, peaceful assemblage and petitioning the government for a redress of grievances. . . .

Long live the Constitution of the United States! Long live the Republic![5]

Other Supreme Court Cases

A number of other cases regarding freedom of speech reached the Supreme Court. These causes helped define free speech law.

Abrams v. ***United States*** *(1919)*. A group of five Russian citizens living in the United States were convicted under the amendment to the 1917 Espionage Act. They had criticized President Wilson in two leaflets and urged workers to strike; the Supreme Court upheld their conviction. The majority used the test of "bad tendency" in upholding the convictions. This doctrine says someone can be convicted if he is *suspected* of doing something wrong. Bad tendency allows government to punish speech that has a tendency to create problems in the future.

Justices Holmes and Brandeis dissented, saying that the clear and present danger test was more appropriate than the bad tendency test. A person has more freedom of speech when the clear and present danger test is applied than when the bad tendency doctrine is used. In the *Abrams* case, the court ruled that the immigrants had taken their freedom too far, by urging Americans to quit supporting their troops and to "arise and put down by force the government of the United States."[6]

Branzburg v. ***Hayes*** *(1972)*. This case involved three appeals concerning the issue of reporters'

The United States instituted its first military draft during World War I, and opposition was widespread. Shown here are men under armed guard because they were on the streets without their draft registration cards.

privileges. Branzburg, a staff reporter for the *Courier-Journal*, a daily newspaper in Louisville, Kentucky, had written two stories about drugs. Branzburg had interviewed drug dealers and users and had promised to keep their identities confidential. Branzburg was subpoenaed by grand juries and refused to answer questions. In this case, the Supreme Court held that reporters cannot refuse to testify in court against those they have reported on. The process of news gathering is protected, but the reporter is not. This was the first case that stated that the freedom to gather news was as important as the freedom to publish.[7] However, a reporter who has information about a case can be forced to testify. A three-part test was a result of this case. First, the journalist must know something relevant to the case. Second, the government must not be able to get the information from other sources. Third, there must be compelling interest in the information. But grand juries are limited as well; they must operate within the limits of the First Amendment as well as reporters.

Justice White said that reporters, like other citizens, must do their duty and testify in court if needed because society has a right to hear all evidence. White rejected the argument that if reporters were forced to testify, their sources would not tell them things anymore. The judges were reluctant to create a privilege for reporters because it could create other problems: Who would qualify as a reporter? Who would oversee the system? By establishing this three-part test, the Court ensured that grand juries could not abuse power by forcing journalists to testify if it was not necessary.

Epperson v. ***Arkansas*** *(1968)*. A teacher challenged a law against teaching evolution in public schools. The Court ruled the law unconstitutional. Tax-supported schools cannot censor the teaching of scientific fact, regardless of the religious beliefs of the community. This case supports constitutional protection for scientific speech and illustrates freedom of speech and of religion. The Court did not say that a particular religion had to be accepted by students in Arkansas. It did say that science teachers had a right to teach without the interference of religion.[8]

Brandenburg v. ***Ohio*** *(1969)*. Clarence Brandenburg, a Ku Klux Klan leader in Ohio, gave a speech warning of "revengeance" against the president, the Congress, and the Supreme Court. He was convicted under Ohio's Criminal Syndicalism Act. The Supreme Court unanimously overturned his conviction. The rule established by this case was that the government had to prove real danger and that threatening speech can be protected unless it incites violence.[9]

Gertz v. ***Welch*** *(1974)*. Elmer Gertz, an attorney, was defamed by a periodical that erroneously claimed he had Communist connections. He sued the periodical and won, but the trial judge ruled he was entitled to no payment. The Supreme Court sided with Gertz and ordered a new trial. This dispute lasted almost thirteen years and changed defamation law.[10]

chapter 8

Free Speech Today

Benjamin Franklin once said, "those willing to give up liberty for security are deserving of neither."[1] The issue of free speech today is more controversial than ever. After centuries of debate, laws, and court decisions, you would think this topic would be resolved. Instead, we now face another world—the world of cyberspace—plus a very different society following the terrorist attacks of September 11, 2001. Supreme Court Justice Benjamin Cardozo wrote in 1937 that free speech is "the indispensable condition of nearly every other form of freedom."[2] Speech is necessary for citizens to discuss topics. Without freedom of speech, other freedoms are compromised. Some feel the right to free speech is being limited, in the name of security. Others are willing to give up some personal freedoms in order to feel safer. How do you feel about this issue?

Libraries and Free Speech

One of the biggest debates surrounds obscenity and pornography accessible to minors online. Libraries are under fire for lack of controls and filters on their online computers, where minors can look up pornographic and obscene material. Some feel libraries need strict filters so that no offensive material can be seen on library computers. Alice Meister, Director of the Bozeman Public Library, in Bozeman, Montana, disagrees. The Internet policy for the Bozeman Library states that the "public library does not serve *in loco parentis*"—that is, the library is not a substitute for parental responsibility. Parents should accompany their children and be part of their online learning. Also under the library policy, all Internet information and resources are available to all patrons; the library does not monitor any information a patron accesses, nor does it control any of the content of any online site.[3]

However, some subtle ways that the Bozeman Library protects kids is to give all patrons a choice of filters. Parents can choose a filter they feel comfortable with. The library is considered a safe haven for kids, and the computers in the children's section automatically come up with the kids' library home page. The Internet terminals are near the desk of the librarian, who can monitor the computers by walking around while children are surfing the Web.[4]

The Communications Decency Act (CDA) was passed in 1996 to ban the transmission of obscene or indecent materials on the Internet. The CDA was ruled unconstitutional, but the debate is not over. One additional effect of the Court's judgment on this law is that the Internet may provide some of the strongest support for the marketplace argument. Because the Internet is largely unregulated and speech is free on the Internet, ideas compete. The best ideas win because individuals have the same access to consumers as a large corporation.[5]

The Internet began in 1969 in a very different form from what we know today. It was an experiment, linking military computers with defense contractors and universities that did research for the military. It branched out to include other academic interests, private citizens, and corporations, and eventually became what it is today. It is an always-changing "web" of places to find information.

Some people see the Internet as potentially harmful. It is an anonymous entity, which makes it easier to distribute things like pornography to minors and others who do not wish to see it. There is no controlling body to regulate what goes where.

Since the Internet has a huge audience, it is feared that any harm stemming from speech will increase as the number of Internet users increases. Many believe antisocial behavior is reinforced by the Internet because it is anonymous.[6] Add to that the problem of parents dropping off their children at the local library for extended periods of time, while they go elsewhere. The library is not a child-care service or a surrogate parent. When parents do not supervise their children's Internet access, the opportunity for children to view objectionable

Laws concerning the use of filters in libraries attempt to balance people's need for information with the need to protect young people from objectionable material.

material increases. Alice Meister sees children left at the library often, which puts the library staff in a difficult position. They are not responsible for monitoring these children or what they view on the computers.[7]

The issue of censorship has not left the library either. Some people take offense at some books offered in libraries. Who makes the decision to keep a book in a library and who can remove it? According to Robert S. Peck, author of *Libraries, The First Amendment, and Cyberspace*, if someone removes a book from a library because he does not like what is in the book, he is violating the First Amendment.[8] Just because your beliefs do not agree with the content of a library book does not give you the right to remove the opportunity to read that book from someone else. At the Bozeman Library, some patrons objected to a young adult magazine because of certain ads. Rather than remove the magazine, the staff relocated it to the downstairs section, away from the children's section.[9]

Free Speech Issues on the Internet

Another issue of concern, particularly in the wake of September 11, 2001, are Web sites that promote and encourage the overthrow of the American government and support those who advocate terrorism and violence. There are hundreds, if not thousands, of Web sites devoted to hate and extremist groups.[10] These hate groups provide links to one another's sites and advocate only one opinion: their own.[11] There is the danger that people visiting these sites will not be well informed. They may hear just one side of an argument and form their opinion based on that. Many times, these sites spread rumors and outright lies, which can lead to hysteria.[12] There are also sites that offer bomb-making instructions, which can lead directly to violence. The free speech issue is safety versus someone's right to disseminate or access information.

Chat rooms, cyber places where people can vent their feelings and find others who share their opinions, are fodder for lawsuits. For example, a man posted a message in which he complained of bad service from a pet supply warehouse. The owner of the store sued the man, saying his company was damaged by the comments. He also sued the host of the chat room, seeking several million dollars in damages. The issue was settled when those sued chose not to spend thousands of dollars to defend themselves in court. The free speech issue was that those sued felt the pet store owner was using money to suppress their opinions. The owner felt he was the victim of a conspiracy against his business.[13] The Internet is bringing up issues that current laws have not yet addressed, for example, whether Web sites are responsible for comments posted to them.

The First Amendment guarantees many freedoms, that some interpret as a freedom of the mind. You are allowed to think whatever thoughts you wish and convey those thoughts to others.[14] It is estimated that about 200 million people have access to the Internet.[15] Because online communication is relatively new, legal ramifications are still being worked out. Some believe that all online speech should be protected. Some feel there need to be more restrictions online than in other forms of media.[16] Since chat rooms are available to all, one solution would be to monitor those chat rooms that are considered dangerous or have the potential to house terrorists. The drawback? Time and money for such monitoring.[17]

When people discuss issues in the real world, they are forced to look at various sides. In the virtual world, people can insulate themselves against a view that they do not agree with. This leads to what is called fragmented speech.[18] People are not exposed to any opposing speech when they choose similar Web sites. They limit the speech they hear. People can also choose to do this in the real world, by reading only one newspaper or watching the same television news channel every day. But a newspaper or news show will generally report all sides of an issue. Not all

Web sites cover differing views. According to Cass Sunstein, author of *republic.com*, those who created the Constitution believed that all citizens had a duty to participate in politics, and one of the ways to do that today is to discuss issues freely.[19] Does this happen on the Internet?

Free Speech and the News

Politicians are famous for twisting words to put a "spin" on events. Think about election years and how every candidate interprets each loss/win in his own way. Think about how news outlets, like papers and television, spin stories. Ideally, news anchors do not offer their views when reporting the news, but it does happen. What about the politicians whose words are twisted without their knowledge or consent? Are their First Amendment rights being stepped on if their words are used out of context? What about outright lies by politicians and lobbyists? Can anything be done to reform this type of speech without infringing on the First Amendment?

Political Campaigns: A Question of Free Speech?

Do you think politicians should have limits placed on how much money they can spend on campaigns? Or do you think a politician should be allowed to spend as much money as he can? Should methods of fund-raising be studied? How do politicians get their money, and who do they get it from?

Politicians are also famous for spending huge amounts of money, which has led to support for campaign financing reform in order to equalize the political arena. People contribute money to those candidates who they believe will promote the causes they support.[20] Why is this a First Amendment issue? Some feel only the candidates who receive the most contributions have an opportunity to get their message to the voters, so only those with lots of money for advertising will be recognized by voters.

Critics of campaign finance reform laws say that they are in violation of the First Amendment because there should be no limits to speech. Limiting finances limits speech. They see the reformers as similar to Robin Hood in the political world, trying to take away the right to speak from the wealthier candidates in order to protect what the candidates with less money want to say.[21] Critics believe reform would limit supporters of a candidate as well as the candidate. Limiting the amount a person can contribute to a candidate would limit supporters' rights to express their beliefs or opinions.

One way to achieve reform is to limit the total amount of money a candidate can spend on his campaign. This gives each candidate the opportunity to spend similar amounts of money in whatever ways he chooses (television ads, mailings, radio spots, rallies, etc.). Critics feel this restricts freedom of expression by limiting the amount of exposure a candidate has.[22]

Another way to promote campaign fairness is to limit the amount a person can contribute to a candidate. Inequality between candidates is less likely to take place because even the wealthy cannot contribute huge amounts of money to "buy" a candidate. It also means that candidates have to obtain their money from a greater number of people, which some proponents feel is a good way to gauge if a politician is truly garnering support of the people who will elect him. Critics feel that this would take too much time away from campaigning, by forcing candidates to spend more time obtaining finances.[23]

Terrorism: A Challenge to Free Speech?

American society changed on September 11, 2001. On that day, American soil was attacked by terrorists. Thousands of innocent people died. Terror, rage, and fear became a part of our routine as an anthrax scare followed within weeks. We must be careful not to repeat history. Following the attack on Pearl Harbor, our government interned over 110,000 people of Japanese descent, simply because of their ancestry. Two thirds of these people were American citizens by birth.[24] Those interned were deprived of their right to free speech because they were never given the opportunity to defend themselves in court. We are faced with a similar situation. Fear and hysteria of Arab-looking people has grown, and suggestions similar to the Japanese-American internment have been posed. Will the same thing happen today?

David Cole and James X. Dempsey, authors of *Terrorism and the Constitution: Sacrificing Civil Liberties in the Name of National Security*, suggest not overreacting while afraid. They fear freedoms will be taken away without just cause, particularly to certain ethnic populations. If that happens, they say, the United States will be sacrificing its democratic foundation.[25]

The USA PATRIOT Act was discussed in chapter 5. It makes sure we have enough military protection on our borders, makes it harder for criminals to launder money, allows law enforcement and intelligence agencies (FBI, CIA) to share information, and processes visas differently. It also allows greater electronic surveillance by the government.[26]

This act has affected our society in numerous ways since its passage. Some critics point to the negative aspects of this law: It is very secret, allows the government to detain immigrants on suspicion, and allows searches and wiretaps without showing probable cause.[27] There is a secret court, FISA, formed under the Foreign Intelligence Surveillance Act, that decides whether to issue search warrants and warrants for electronic eavesdropping and wiretapping. Its purpose is to collect foreign intelligence information to protect the United States from foreign spies. Under Section 215, libraries are required to provide information about their patrons and their reading and online habits to the FBI if they want to continue receiving federal funding. Libraries are not allowed to tell people their records have been accessed, so no one knows whether or not he or she is being watched.

Many liken the Patriot Act to the witch hunts of the McCarthy era.[28] Others feel the act is necessary, now that terrorists have invaded America with their brutal tactics. The Bozeman Library has noticed no change in Internet usage since the passage of this act. And the only change this library made was to invite an Islamic family to give some programs to educate the community.[29]

Does this law violate civil liberties? Or as citizens, are we willing to give up some liberty in exchange for security? Each person must answer for himself. Justice Sandra Day O'Connor has said, "We're likely to experience more restrictions on personal freedom than has ever been the case in this country."[30] Justice Ruth Bader Ginsburg argued, "If we gave up our freedom as the price of security, we would no longer be the great nation we are."[31] When Supreme Court justices cannot agree on the future of the First Amendment, it causes anxiety for citizens. As we continue to shape our future and that of our freedom of speech, each of us will be part of an ongoing history.

chapter 9

Moot Court: Your Turn to Debate

In this chapter, you will learn how to participate in a mock judicial proceeding of your own. One type of court exercise is called "moot court." A moot court is a dramatization of a hypothetical (fictitious) or real case that went before an appeals court or the Supreme Court. The purpose of these courts is to rule on a lower court's decision. It is different from a trial in that no witnesses appear and testify, just as no witnesses are called in a Supreme Court case. Also, the focus is on whether the court below made any mistakes, rather than on finding all the facts of a case.

In moot court, the players take the roles of judges, clerks, attorneys, and journalists. They do research, write briefs, and argue legal issues before a make-believe panel of appeals court judges. The exercise hones research, writing, and debate skills.

Taking part in a moot court is a fun way to get a feeling for how a real court case occurs. Try a moot court activity with your class or club.[1] Here's how.

Step 1: Assign Roles

Here are the roles you will need to fill:

◇ Judges. If the group is large enough, have nine justices like the Supreme Court has. Otherwise, have a panel of three appellate court judges. Choose one person to be Chief Justice and direct the proceeding. The judges hear the attorneys' arguments, question them, and then write and deliver the final ruling. The court's majority opinion is the position agreed upon by a majority of the panel. Individual judges may choose to issue concurring or dissenting opinions of their own.

◇ Two or more court clerks. They work with the judges to prepare five or more questions to ask the attorneys during oral arguments. Judicial clerks also help with research for judges' opinions.

◇ A team of two or more attorneys for the appellant. They feel the lower court was wrong.

◇ A team of two or more attorneys for the appellee. They believe the lower court ruled correctly.

◇ A designated spokesperson to present the argument (though any of the attorneys can answer questions from the judges). Attorneys must address the major issues by presenting the most persuasive arguments for their side.

◇ Two or more reporters. They interview the attorneys before the case and write news stories about the facts of the case and the final ruling.

◇ The bailiff, who calls the court to order. The bailiff will also time each side's oral argument.

Step 2: Prepare Your Case

Part 1: Gather Information

The case you will hear and decide will be *Bethel School District* v. *Fraser* (1986). To review: A high school senior delivered a speech at a school-sponsored assembly that was run by the students. Matthew Fraser used sexual humor in his speech, which offended teachers and many students.

> I know a man who's firm—he's firm in his pants, he's firm in his shirt, his character is firm—but most of all, his belief in you, the students of Bethel, is firm.
>
> Jeff Kuhlman is a man who takes his point and pounds it in. If necessary, he'll take an issue and nail it to the wall. He doesn't attack things in spurts—he drives hard, pushing and pushing until finally—he succeeds.
>
> Jeff is a man who will go to the very end—even the climax, for each and every one of you.
>
> So vote for Jeff for A.S.B. vice-president—he'll never come between you and the best our high school can be.

Other students became unruly, calling out things and simulating sexual actions. Fraser was suspended for three days. He was also taken off the list to be a graduation speaker. The school based his punishment on a rule that states "conduct which materially and substantially interferes with the educational process is prohibited, including the use of obscene, profane language or gestures."[2] Fraser sued authorities, saying his First Amendment rights had been violated.

The district court ruled in Fraser's favor, saying the school's rule was vague and overbroad. In the meantime, he was elected graduation speaker and delivered the commencement address. The school district appealed to the U.S. circuit court, which also ruled in Fraser's favor because the school could not prove the assembly was disrupted by Fraser's speech. The school authorities took the case to the Supreme Court.

Part 2: Write Your Briefs

A legal brief is a written presentation of your argument. Brainstorm with the lawyers on your team. Which arguments are strongest for you? What are your weaknesses?

You may want to divide up arguments for research and writing. If so, be sure to work as a team to put the brief together. Otherwise, your brief may have holes or read poorly.

Use these arguments as suggestions, and think of arguments of your own that might sway the opinion of the court in your favor.

Appellant's team (Bethel School District): Matthew Fraser violated school policy by using vulgar speech at a school-sponsored assembly. If Fraser is allowed to use this type of speech, where does the school draw the line? He knowingly used this speech to a captive audience, most of whom were embarrassed and did not want to listen to it. His speech served no purpose to education. Schools are places for learning, and the only ones able to make the judgment as to what speech is appropriate are school officials.

Appellee's team (Matthew Fraser): Fraser's speech was not technically obscene speech. His free speech rights were violated by the suspension because the students who did not want to listen could have left the assembly. The assembly was student run. It was a nominating speech for a friend. He was trying to be funny and draw attention to the election. His speech did not hinder education at the school.

In real life, court rules spell out what briefs must contain. Use these rules for your moot court activity:

1. The cover page should have the case name, *Bethel School District* v. *Fraser*. Say whether it

is the case for the appellant or the appellee. List the lawyers' names.

2. The text of the brief should have these sections:

   A. Statement of the issue for review: What question is before the court?

   B. Statement of the case: What is this case about? How did the trial court rule?

   C. Statement of the facts: Briefly describe the facts relevant to the case.

   D. Summary of the argument: Sum up your argument in 150 words or less.

   E. Argument: Spell out the legal arguments that support your side. You can split this into sections with subheadings for each part. Include references to cases or authorities that help your side.

   F. Conclusion: Ask the court to rule for your client.

3. Real appeals briefs may be thirty pages long. Limit your brief to no more than five typed pages, double-spaced, or about 1,250 words. If possible, type on a computer. Otherwise, write *very* neatly.

4. On an agreed-upon date, each team gives the other side a copy of its brief. Each judge gets a copy too. If you do this in class, give the teacher a copy. Be sure each team member keeps a copy of the brief too.

   In real life, lawyers often prepare reply briefs.

They answer points made by the other side. You won't do that. But you should be ready to answer their points in oral argument.

Part 3: Prepare for Oral Argument
Judges should read all the briefs before oral argument. They should prepare questions for the lawyers.

Each side will have up to fifteen minutes to argue its case.

Step 3: Hold the Oral Argument

Part 1: Assemble the Participants

- ◇ The judges sit together at the front of the room. This is the bench. They should not enter until the bailiff calls the court to order. A speaking podium or lectern faces the bench.

- ◇ The appellant's team of attorneys sits at one side, facing the judges.

- ◇ The appellee's team sits at the opposite side, also facing the judges.

- ◇ The reporters sit at the back.

- ◇ As the judges enter, the bailiff calls the court to order: "Oyez (oy-yay)! Oyez! Oyez! The _____ court of the United States is now in session with the Honorable Chief Justice ____ presiding. All will stand and remain standing until the judges are seated and the Chief Justice has asked all present to be seated."

Part 2: Present the Case

◇ The Chief Justice calls the case and asks whether the parties are ready. Each team's spokesperson answers "Yes."

◇ The appellant's spokesperson approaches the podium saying, "May it please the court." Then argument begins. Judges interrupt when they wish to ask a question. The attorneys respectfully answer any questions as asked. Don't get flustered if a judge interrupts with a question. Answer the question honestly. Then move on.

◇ Then the appellee's team takes its turn.

◇ Each team has up to fifteen minutes to present its argument. If the appellant's team wants, it can save five minutes of its time to rebut the appellee's argument. If so, the spokesperson should inform the court before sitting down.

◇ After the arguments, the bailiff tells everyone to rise as the judges leave to debate their decision.

◇ At this time, reporters may interview lawyers for the parties and begin working on their articles.

◇ After an agreed-upon time, the judges return and present their ruling, announced by the Chief Justice.

Part 3: Publish and Report

◇ A few days later, the court's majority opinion is made available in written form, along with any dissenting opinions and individual concurring opinions.

◇ At the same time, the reporters' stories are made available.

Questions for Discussion

1. Should symbolic acts, such as flag burning, be protected by the First Amendment? What is the difference between a symbolic act and an act of desecration?

2. Has the United States gone too far in trying to protect the right of free speech and, by doing so, failed to protect citizens from more dangerous problems?

3. Should the Internet be regulated? If you believe that it should be, how should regulation be accomplished?

4. Do you think our present form of free speech is what the Founding Fathers intended?

5. What limits would you place on free speech, if any? What freedoms would you be willing to give up?

Chapter Notes

Chapter 1. What Is Free Speech?

1. Thomas L. Tedford and Dale A. Herbeck, *Freedom of Speech in the United States* (State College, Pa.: Strata Publishing, Inc., 2001), pp. 302–306.

2. Ibid., p. 303.

3. Linda R. Monk, *The Words We Live By* (New York: Stonesong Press Book, 2003), p. 137.

4. Ibid., p. 127.

5. Ibid., p. 146.

6. Jerome A. Barron, *Freedom of the Press For Whom?* (Bloomington, Ind.: Indiana University Press, 1973), pp. 319–321.

7. John E. Semonche, *Charting the Future* (Westport, Conn.: Greenwood Press, 1978), p. 205.

8. *Schenck* v. *United States, Baer* v. *United States*, 249 U.S. 52 (1919).

9. Nat Hentoff, *Free Speech for Me—But Not for Thee* (New York: HarperCollins, 1992), pp. 18–20.

10. Gail Schontzler, "'Nigger' author examines word's history," *Bozeman Daily Chronicle*, January 23, 2004, p. A3.

11. Monk, p. 117.

12. Ibid., p. 92.

13. John Wirenius, *First Amendment, First Principles* (New York: Holmes & Meier, 2000), p. 225.

14. Monk, p. 145.

Chapter 2. History of Free Speech

1. Samuel Noah Kramer, *The Sumerians: Their History, Culture, and Character* (Chicago: University of Chicago Press, 1971), p. 82.

2. Ibid., p. 82.

3. Thomas L. Tedford and Dale A. Herbeck, *Freedom of Speech in the United States* (State College, Pa.: Strata Publishing, Inc., 2001), p. 4.

4. Norman F. Cantor, *Civilization of the Middle Ages* (New York: Harper Perennial, 1994), pp. 40–41.

5. Tedford and Herbeck, p. 13.

6. Robert Hargreaves, *The First Freedom: A History of Free Speech* (Phoenix Mill, England: Sutton Publishing, 2002), p. 101.

7. Bailey Stone, *Reinterpreting the French Revolution* (Cambridge, England: Cambridge University Press, 2002), pp. 117–118.

8. Linda R. Monk, *The Words We Live By* (New York: Stonesong Press Book, 2003), pp. 146–147.

9. Ibid., p. 147.

Chapter 3. Free Speech Should Be Unrestricted: Arguments for Free Speech

1. Lee C. Bollinger and Geoffrey R. Stone, eds., *Eternally Vigilant: Free Speech in the Modern Era* (Chicago: University of Chicago Press, 2002), p. 107.

2. Thomas L. Tedford and Dale A. Herbeck, *Freedom of Speech in the United States* (State College, Pa.: Strata Publishing, Inc., 2001), p. 420.

3. Ibid.

4. Jerome A. Barron and C. Thomas Dienes, *First Amendment Law in a Nutshell* (St. Paul, Minn.: West Group, 2000), p. 87.

5. Ibid., p. 85.

6. Tedford and Herbeck, p. 170.

7. Ibid., p. 171.

8. Donald Alexander Downs, *Nazis in Skokie* (Notre Dame, Ind.: University of Notre Dame Press, 1985), pp. 10–11.

9. John Wirenius, *First Amendment, First Principles* (New York: Holmes & Meier, 2000), p. 116.

10. Robert Hargreaves, *The First Freedom: A History of Free Speech* (Phoenix Mill, England: Sutton Publishing, 2002), pp. 220–225.

11. Tedford and Herbeck, p. 416.

12. Wirenius, pp. 324–325.

13. John Stuart Mill, *On Liberty* (London: Penguin, 1974, reprint), pp. 119–140.

14. Jerome A. Barron, *Freedom of the Press For Whom?* (Bloomington, Ind.: Indiana University Press, 1973), pp. 319–322.

15. Lucas A. Powe, Jr., *The Warren Court and American Politics* (Cambridge, Mass.: Belknap Press, 2000), p. 144.

16. Greg LaMotte and Patty Davis, "Oprah: 'Free Speech rocks'," *CNN.com*, February 26, 1998, <http://www.cnn.com/US/9802/26/oprah.verdict/> (October 1, 2003).

17. Ibid.

18. Barbara Wartelle Wall, "Legal Watch: Court of Appeals Agrees That Oprah Winfrey Did Not Libel Beef," *Gannet News Watch*, March 10, 2000, <http://www.gannett.com/go/newswatch/2000/march/mw0310-5.htm> (October 1, 2003).

19. John W. Gonzalez, "New Beef With Oprah: Irate Cattlemen Across America Are Suing Talk Show Host Over Disparaging Comments," *Houston Chronicle*, April 26, 1998, p. Al.

20. "Stockmen's Suit Against Oprah Is Dismissed," *Houston Chronicle*, September 18, 2002, p. A25.

21. Tedford and Herbeck, pp. 418–419.

22. Archibald Cox, *The Court and the Constitution* (Boston: Houghton Mifflin, 1987), p. 214.

23. Tedford and Herbeck, p. 447.

24. Barron and Dienes, pp. 73–74.

25. Wirenius, p. 221.

26. Barron and Dienes, pp. 95–98.

27. Ibid., p. 97.

28. Cox, p. 212.

29. Tedford and Herbeck, p. 418.

30. Ibid.

31. Cass R. Sunstein, *Democracy and the Problem of Free Speech* (New York: The Free Press, 1993), p. 122.

32. Cass Sunstein, *republic.com* (Princeton, N.J.: Princeton University Press, 2001), p. 39.

33. Barron and Dienes, pp. 125–126.

34. Sunstein, *republic.com*, p. 41.

35. Ibid., p. 201.

36. *Whitney* v. *People of the State of California*, 274 U.S. 357 (1927).

37. Barron and Dienes, p. 15.

38. Wirenius, p. 319.

39. Donald Alexander Downs, *Nazis in Skokie* (Notre Dame, Ind.: University of Notre Dame Press, 1985), pp. 76–77.

40. Ibid., p. 13.

41. Phillipa Strum, *When the Nazis Came to Skokie: Freedom for Speech We Hate* (Lawrence, Kans.: University Press of Kansas, 1999), pp. 141–143.

Chapter 4. Free Speech Needs Limits: Arguments Against Free Speech

1. John F. Wirenius, *First Amendment, First Principles* (New York: Holmes & Meier, 2000), p. 316.

2. Stanley Fish, *There's No Such Thing As Free Speech* (New York: Oxford University Press, 1994), p. 110.

3. Jerome A. Barron and C. Thomas Dienes, *First Amendment Law* (St. Paul, Minn.: West Publishing Group, 2000), pp. 7–8.

4. Thomas L. Tedford and Dale A. Herbeck, *Freedom of Speech in the United States* (State College, Pa.: Strata Publishing, Inc., 2001), p. 423.

5. Ibid., pp. 176–177.

6. Barron and Dienes, p. 198.

7. Ibid., p. 234.

8. Wirenius, p. 149–150.

9. Barron and Dienes, p. 11.

10. Tedford and Herbeck, p. 51.

11. "Regulation of Obscenity & Indecent Speech," *Exploring Constitutional Conflicts*, n.d., <http://www.law.umkc.edu/faculty/projects/ftrials/bruce/bruceindecentspeech.htm> (November 21, 2004).

12. Donald Alexander Downs, *Nazis in Skokie* (Notre Dame, Ind.: University of Notre Dame Press, 1985), p. 1.

13. Ibid., pp. 131–132, 155, 158.

14. Ibid., pp. 85–93.

15. Phillipa Strum, *When the Nazis Came to Skokie: Freedom for Speech We Hate* (Lawrence, Kans.: University Press of Kansas, 1999), p. 115.

16. Ibid., pp. 116–118.

17. Barron and Dienes, pp. 321–322.

18. Tedford and Herbeck, p. 301.

19. Barron and Dienes, pp. 322–323.

20. Bob Anez, "Montana Supreme Court rules 'fighting words' can be a crime," *The Missoulian*, December 23, 2003, <http://www.missoulian.com/articles/2003/12/23/news/mtregional/zznews06.prt> (January 21, 2005).

Chapter 5. Laws of Our Land

1. Thomas L. Tedford and Dale A. Herbeck, *Freedom of Speech in the United States* (State College, Pa.: Strata Publishing, Inc., 2001), p. 25.

2. Ibid.

3. Robert Hargreaves, *The First Freedom: A History of Free Speech* (Phoenix Mill, England: Sutton Publishing, 2002), p. 179.

4. Michael Kent Curtis, *Free Speech, "The People's Darling Privilege"* (Durham, N.C.: Duke University Press, 2000), pp. 59–62.

5. Ibid., pp. 77–79.

6. Hargreaves, p. 187.

7. Charles F. Patterson, *The True Meaning of the Constitution* (Xenia, Ohio: Bentham Press, 2002), pp. 233–234.

8. Tedford and Herbeck, p. 47.

9. Linda R. Monk, *The Words We Live By* (New York: Stonesong Press Book, 2003), p. 139.

10. Tedford and Herbeck, p. 59.

11. Ibid., p. 68.

12. Maria Newman and Adam Liptak, "Times Reporter Is Held in Contempt in Leak Inquiry," October 7, 2004, <http://www.nytimes.com/2004/10/07/national/07CND-MILLER.html> (January 21, 2005).

13. Lee C. Bollinger and Geoffrey R. Stone, eds., *Eternally Vigilant: Free Speech in the Modern Era* (Chicago: University of Chicago Press, 2002), pp. 267–270.

14. Tedford and Herbeck, pp. 372–374.

15. "The case for the Communications Decency Act," *CNNinteractive*, February 16, 2003, <http://www.cnn.com/US/9703/cda.scotus/for/index.html> (January 21, 2005).

16. "The Communications Decency Act Defined," *CNNinteractive*, February 15, 2003, <http://www.cnn.com/US/9703/cda.scotus/what.is.cda/index.html> (January 21, 2005).

17. John F. Wirenius, *First Amendment, First Principles* (New York: Holmes & Meier, 2000), pp. 199–200.

18. Jerome A. Barron and C. Thomas Dienes, *First Amendment Law* (St. Paul, Minn.: West Publishing Group, 2000), pp. 40, 46.

19. Ibid., p. 120.

20. Tedford and Herbeck, p. 391.

21. Wirenius, p. 221.

22. "The case against the Communications Decency Act," *CNNinteractive*, February 16, 2003, <http://www.cnn.com/US/9703/cda.scotus/against/index.html> (January 21, 2005).

23. Barron and Dienes, pp. 117–120.

24. Tedford and Herbeck, p. 396.

25. David Cole and James X. Dempsey, *Terrorism and the Constitution: Sacrificing Civil Liberties in the Name of National Security* (New York: The New Press, 2002), pp. 151–153, 161–162.

26. "Clash Over Patriot Act," *CBSNews.com*, June 5, 2003, <http://www.cbsnews.com/stories/2003/06/05/attack/printable;557086.shtml> (June 14, 2003).

27. "Ashcroft Touts Patriot Act," *Wired News*, August 19, 2003, <http://wired.com/news/conflict/0,2100,60102,00.html> (November 18, 2004).

28. From the USA Patriot Act

29. Dan Eggen, "Key Part of Patriot Act Ruled Unconstitutional," *Washington Post*, September 30, 2004, <http://www.washingtonpost.com/wp-dyn/articles?A59626-2004Sep29.html> (November 18, 2004).

Chapter 6. According to the Courts

1. Raoul Berger, *Congress v. The Supreme Court* (Cambridge, Mass.: Harvard University Press, 1969), pp. 48–49, 199.

2. Robert Justin Goldstein, *Flag Burning & Free Speech* (Lawrence, Kans.: University Press of Kansas, 2000), p. 52.

3. Ibid., p. 102.

4. Ibid., p. 106.

5. Ibid., p. 107.

6. Ibid.

7. Charles F. Patterson, *The True Meaning of the Constitution* (Xenia, Ohio: Bentham Press, 2002), p. 237.

8. Goldstein, pp. 109, 114–115.

9. Jerome A. Barron and C. Thomas Dienes, *First Amendment Law* (St. Paul, Minn.: West Group, 2000), pp. 88–90.

10. John F. Wirenius, *First Amendment, First Principles* (New York: Holmes & Meier, 2000), p. 91.

11. Ibid., p. 92.

12. Barron and Dienes, p. 84.

13. Stanley Fish, *There's No Such Thing As Free Speech* (New York: Oxford University Press, 1994), pp. 105–106.

14. John W. Johnson, *The Struggle For Student Rights: Tinker v. Des Moines and the 1960's* (Lawrence, Kans.: University Press of Kansas, 1997), pp. 170–171.

15. Eve H. Malakoff and Mark S. Wisiniewski, eds., *First Amendment and The Schools* (Washington, D.C.:

National School Boards Association Council of School Attorneys, 1983), p. 59.

16. Barron and Dienes, p. 78.

17. Wirenius, pp. 115–117.

18. "Legal Opinions Relating to Obscenity Prosecutions of Comedian Lenny Bruce," *Famous Trials: The Lenny Bruce Trial*, n.d., <http://www.law.umkc.edu/faculty/projects/ftrials/bruce/brucecourtdecisions.html> (November 21, 2004).

Chapter 7. The Supreme Court's Judgment

1. Raoul Berger, *Congress v. The Supreme Court* (Cambridge, Mass.: Harvard University Press, 1969), p. 300.

2. John E. Semonche, *Charting the Future* (Westport, Conn.: Greenwood Press, 1978), p. 365.

3. Archibald Cox, *The Court and the Constitution* (Boston: Houghton Mifflin, 1987), p. 219.

4. John F. Wirenius, *First Amendment, First Principles* (New York: Holmes & Meier, 2000), p. 37.

5. "Assert Your Rights!" *1st Amendment Online*, n.d., <http://1stam.umn.edu/archive/primary/schenck.pdf> (March 22, 2005).

6. Wirenius, p. 43.

7. Jerome A. Barron and C. Thomas Dienes, *First Amendment* Law (St. Paul, Minn.: West Group, 2000), p. 373.

8. Thomas L. Tedford and Dale A. Herbeck, *Freedom of Speech in the United States* (State College, Pa.: Strata Publishing, Inc., 2001), pp. 125–126.

9. "Advocacy of Unlawful Action and the 'Incitement Test,'" *Exploring Constitutional Conflicts*, n.d., <http://www.law.umkc.edu/faculty/projects/ftrials/conlaw/incitement.htm> (November 22, 2004).

10. Tedford and Herbeck, p. 94.

Chapter 8. Free Speech Today

1. Martin Garbus, *Courting Disaster* (New York: Times Books, 2002), p. 287.

2. Robert S. Peck, *Libraries, The First Amendment, and Cyberspace* (Chicago: American Library Association, 2000), pp. 2–3.

3. Personal interview with Alice Meister, March 5, 2004.

4. Ibid.

5. John F. Wirenius, *First Amendment, First Principles* (New York: Holmes & Meier, 2000), p. 222.

6. Lee C. Bollinger and Geoffrey R. Stone, eds., *Eternally Vigilant: Free Speech in the Modern Era* (Chicago: University of Chicago Press, 2002), pp. 150–151.

7. Personal interview with Alice Meister, March 5, 2004.

8. Peck, p. 2.

9. Personal interview with Alice Meister, March 5, 2004.

10. Cass Sunstein, *republic.com* (Princeton, N.J.: Princeton University Press, 2001), p. 62.

11. Ibid., pp. 62–65.

12. Ibid., pp. 52–53.

13. Katherine Mieszkowski, "Free Speech and the Internet: A Fish Story," *Salon.com*, April 14, 2002, <http://www.salon.com/tech/feature/2002/04/04/aquatic_plants/index1.html> (February 21, 2003).

14. Peck, p. 3.

15. Wirenius, p. 195.

16. Ibid., pp. 196–197.

17. Bollinger and Stone, p. 150.

18. Sunstein, p. 53.

19. Ibid., p. 42.

20. Cass R. Sunstein, *Democracy and the Problem of Free Speech* (New York: The Free Press, 1993), p. 94.

21. Ibid., pp. 94–95.

22. Jerome A. Barron and C. Thomas Dienes, *First Amendment Law* (St. Paul, Minn.: West Group, 2000), pp. 281–282.

23. Ibid., pp. 282–283.

24. David Cole and James X. Dempsey, *Terrorism and the Constitution: Sacrificing Civil Liberties in the Name of National Security* (New York: The New Press, 2002), p. 150.

25. Ibid., p. 148.

26. Ibid., p. 152.

27. Ibid., pp. 152–153.

28. Ibid., p. 153.

29. Personal interview with Alice Meister, March 5, 2004.

30. Garbus, p. 287.

31. Ibid.

Chapter 9. Moot Court: Your Turn to Debate

1. Adapted from Millie Aulbur, "Constitutional Issues and Teenagers," *The Missouri Bar*, n.d., <http://www.molbar.org/teach/clesson.htm> (December 10, 2004); Street Law, Inc., and the Supreme Court Historical Society, "Moot Court Activity," 2002, <http://www.landmarkcases.org> (December 10, 2004); with suggestions from Ron Fridell and Kathiann M. Kowalski.

2. Thomas L. Tedford and Dale A. Herbeck, *Freedom of Speech in the United States* (State College, Pa.: Strata Publishing, Inc., 2001), p. 301.

Glossary

actual malice—Knowing something is false and printing it anyway.

bad tendency—A test that allows government to stop any speech that has a tendency to lead to a problem in the future.

broad—An interpretation of the Constitution that allows the government a large degree of flexibility.

censor—To remove or prohibit something believed to be objectionable.

clear and present danger—A test that allows speech to continue until an obvious and immediate danger is present.

common law—Law based on custom.

defamation—Destroying a person's reputation; includes libel and slander.

desecration—Taking away the sacred meaning of something.

freedom of expression—Five of the rights guaranteed by the Constitution—freedom of speech, press, religion, the right to gather peaceably, and the right to petition the government.

hate speech—Speech that uses a person's ethnicity,

race, or religion to incite violence against that person.

indecency—A form of sexually explicit material that is protected by the First Amendment.

lewd—Intended to incite lust, or sexual desire, within a person; often offensive.

libel—A written false statement that harms a person's reputation.

obscenity—A form of sexually explicit material not protected by the First Amendment.

offensive statement—Speech that uses a person's race, ethnicity, or religion, along with insults, to force a reaction from that person.

pornography—Writings or pictures used to arouse sexual desire.

prior restraint—Stopping a message before it is sent.

slander—A spoken false statement that harms a person's reputation.

tolerance—Accepting someone else's beliefs, even though you do not believe the same.

vague—an interpretation that insufficiently defines something so that a person cannot be sure about what is legal and what is not.

Further Reading

Books

Egendorf, Laura K., ed. *Should There Be Limits to Free Speech?* San Diego, Calif.: Greenhaven Press, 2003.

Harer, John B., and Jeanne E. Harrell. *People for and Against Restricted or Free Expression.* Westport, Conn.: Greenwood Press, 2002.

Isler, Claudia. *The Right to Free Speech.* New York: Rosen Publishing Group, 2001.

Kennedy, Sheila Suess, ed. *Free Expression in America: A Documentary History.* Westport, Conn.: Greenwood Press, 1999.

Nardo, Don. *The Bill of Rights.* San Diego, Calif.: Greenhaven Press, 1998.

Pendergast, Tom, Sara Pendergast, and John Sousanis. *Constitutional Amendments: From Freedom of Speech to Flag Burning.* Detroit, Mich.: UXL, 2001.

Internet Addresses

Ben's Guide to the U.S. Government for Kids: The Supreme Court
<http://bensguide.gpo.gov/9-12/government/national/scourt.html>

First Amendment Center
<http://www.firstamendmentcenter.org>

Supreme Court of the United States
<http://www.supremecourtus.gov>

Index